MIDLIFE ORPHAN

MIDLIFE ORPHAN

*Facing Life's Changes
Now That Your Parents Are Gone*

JANE BROOKS

BERKLEY BOOKS, NEW YORK

This book is an original publication of The Berkley Publishing Group.

MIDLIFE ORPHAN

A Berkley Book / published by arrangement with
the author

PRINTING HISTORY
Berkley trade paperback edition / April 1999

The Penguin Putnam Inc. World Wide Web site address is
http://www.penguinputnam.com

ISBN: 0-425-16693-7

BERKLEY®
Berkley Books are published by The Berkley Publishing Group,
a member of Penguin Putnam Inc.,
375 Hudson Street, New York, New York 10014.
BERKLEY and the "B" design
are trademarks belonging to Berkley Publishing Corporation.

PRINTED IN THE UNITED STATES OF AMERICA

10   9   8   7   6   5   4   3   2   1

In memory of my parents, Bert and Leonard Brooks

ACKNOWLEDGMENTS

*I*n second grade when I unwillingly acquired my first pair of glasses, I wrote a "book" about the experience. *Milly's Glasses* was the story of a young girl who loathed her eyeglasses until she discovered their magical powers. I discovered early that there is nothing like writing to process thoughts and feelings.

I suppose the seed for this book was planted more than a dozen years ago when my father was first diagnosed with Alzheimer's disease. Of course, I had no inkling then of the dark years ahead or that I would end up writing about a subject so intensely emotional or personal as the death of my parents. Nor could I have known that in the process, I would undergo dramatic personal turns.

Time, the greatest healer, and writing, always my savior, were the primary agents of change. But also responsible were the many men and women I interviewed whose honesty and openness about their family relationships helped me put my experience with my own family of origin in perspective. Special thanks to those people who opened their hearts in very personal and poignant interviews. If we hadn't agreed upon anonymity, I would proudly name them here.

I am also indebted to the various people who contributed their thoughts and professional expertise, especially to John DeBerry of the Northwestern Memorial Hospice Program (Chicago). Incredibly kind and generous with his time, it is no wonder John is so respected by the many persons he has helped in their bereavement.

Thanks to Carol Mann, my agent, whose support of this project allowed it to become a reality. And I thank my editor, Hillary Cige, for guiding this project with a keen sensitivity to the topic and to the many voices in the book.

Many friends and associates also contributed to this book in less obvious ways. For her astute comments, unwavering support and gentle mentoring, I wish to thank Pat Shapiro. During many long walks, dinners, and phone calls, she offered her help through each stage of this effort. And of course, there are the friends and family members whose caring, constancy and validation have given me the courage to trust my own voice.

Most of all, I am grateful to my sons, Dan and Andy Moskowitz, whose love has sustained and energized me throughout the years. Their genuine enthusiasm and support for this book have been immeasurable. In chapter after chapter, they offered their suggestions, refreshing my memory in some cases and correcting it in others. They magnanimously tolerated my total preoccupation with this project, and indulged my obsession. My harshest critics and my proudest fans, my sons are truly my greatest treasure.

CONTENTS

MIDLIFE ORPHAN

INTRODUCTION

$\mathcal{T}$he summer after my mother died, I spent a couple weeks traveling with a friend through Nova Scotia. We sampled the renowned scallops in Digby, swayed to the droning bagpipes in Antigonish, and attempted to photograph the elusive puffins of Bird Island. As we checked out of a B&B in the picturesque little village of Margaree Harbour, I complimented our hostess, a married woman in her thirties, on her lovely home. She had been busily shoving her child's toys out of our way but she stopped to remark that the house had belonged to her parents, who had died the year before, within six months of each other. Then, looking directly at me with red-rimmed eyes, she said quietly, "I'm an orphan now."

Her words jolted me, for they described precisely how I had been feeling since my mother's death, which came only sixteen months after my father died. It wasn't a sensation I was comfortable sharing. After all, for a forty-seven-year-old mother of two to admit to feeling like an orphan was somewhat embarrassing, making me seem needy and childish, especially since everyone assumed within weeks after the funeral that I was fine. And in many ways, I was. I continued to work, to parent, and to go about my life. Internally, however, something was happening to me. The avalanche of emotions churning inside was throwing me off balance. When I heard this woman's words, I realized that perhaps my reaction wasn't as extreme or unique as I imagined.

Every year more than 11 million adults—5 percent of the population—lose a parent.[1] For many, it is their last parent. In fact, by the time we reach age sixty-two, 75 percent of adults have lost both parents. For the baby boom generation, which comprises one-third of the population of the United States, the loss of parents will become a sad reality in the next decade.

For most people, the death of a loved one leaves unfinished business. But the death of the last parent does so even more, for when the last parent dies we lose a relationship unlike any other in our life. It's no wonder that we feel so bereft. Yet, few of us are prepared for the intensity or the duration of our grief. The death of the last parent, an event that we've known would obviously happen someday, is a shock to our core in ways that we have not anticipated.

When I returned from Nova Scotia, rested and restored, I decided it was time to explore the nature of my orphaned feelings, which previously I had swept under some amorphous mental carpet. Although the loss of my last parent had elicited a tremendous sense of abandonment, it was also, initially, a relief. It meant that two years of shuttling back and forth tending to ailing parents and the ensuing emotional roller coaster ended. Gradually, however, the reality of my situation began to sink in as I made the transition from adult child to adult at the family helm.

When my mother died, friends rallied around, as they had done the year before at my father's death. But with very few peers who had lost both parents, I felt quite alone. Once I began to talk openly about my experience, that changed. I encountered midlife orphans everywhere—at the cheese counter of the local Italian gourmet market; in a clothing boutique in Pittsburgh, where my son attends college; at the neighborhood library; and in the New Hampshire hospital where we ended up spending our summer vacation when my younger son contracted meningitis. Whenever the subject of parental death came up, midlife orphans were eager to talk, because this was a topic we rarely discussed with others. The idea for this book began to brew.

Library research introduced me to journals dedicated solely to the subject of death. I read whatever studies about death and loss were available, studies so specific that some compared the incidence of alcoholism among men in a certain age range who had lost a mother versus a father. Web sites provided links to home pages on grieving and chat rooms where the bereaved can share their feelings. Several good books dealt with losing a parent—I had read most of those when my father died. But losing the last parent was distinctly different from losing the first, and I wasn't finding what I wanted to know—how other adults experienced it. Very little was written about the impact of parental death on midlife adults and barely any research focused exclusively on the impact of the loss of the second parent. Yet it is one of the most common rites of passage of the human experience.

Miriam and Sidney Moss, among the few researchers who have looked at the impact of the loss of parents on middle-age adults, speculate that one reason for the lack of research may be that other concerns of middle age take precedence over the loss of parents.[2] Midlife orphans wrestle with the usual midlife issues—marital relationships, career concerns, personal health, and parent-adolescent conflicts—but they do it against the backdrop of the loss of the family of origin in which they played a central part. Nearly all of the midlife adults I interviewed made a connection between the current issues in their lives and grief over the death of the last parent.

The emotions and changes I was experiencing with the loss of my last parent were uniquely mine simply because my relationship to my parents and my family of origin was unique. This may also explain the lack of research—as the Mosses have suggested, the personal response to the death of parents follows no pattern.[3] But the more I spoke with other midlife orphans, the more similarities I detected, some subtle, others more pronounced. I found that the sense of being orphaned or abandoned is common when the last parent dies. The period after the loss becomes one of introspection and self-evaluation, as issues revolving around our family of origin rear themselves—old sibling rivalries get revived and insecurities and uncertainties are stirred up. And the concerns that confront midlife orphans are weighted with a history of emotions and attitudes. For example, a long-awaited inheritance may finally be ours, but how disconcerting to find that it is attached to complex issues of guilt, sibling rivalry, and mistrust.

As word of my project spread, phone calls and e-mail messages increased ("So-and-so has a friend who's a midlife orphan and would love to talk to you"). So many people volunteered to be interviewed that I couldn't possibly get to everyone. In the end, I spoke with fifty-two midlife orphans in lengthy interviews, lasting from an hour and a half to three hours. Many of these were face-to-face, the rest by phone. I talked to men and women from ages thirty-seven to sixty-two. They were single, married, divorced, parents, childless, and sisters and brothers. All but one grew up with their birth parents; the other was adopted as an infant. They represented many religions—among them were Catholics, Methodists, Quakers, Jews, Baptists, and Presbyterians. Some were very observant, many were loosely affiliated or nonobservant. They were 95 percent Caucasian and 5 percent African-American. They were teachers, social workers, musicians, artists, lawyers, homemakers—primarily college-educated. I interviewed midlife adults from California to New York, from Maine to Florida, from Illinois, Ohio, and Pennsylvania. With the exception of two, the adults I interviewed had lost their last parent within the past seven years. I set this parameter because I wanted to see how our outlook changes from the time our last parent dies through the ensuing years. Because of the candid nature of the interviews, the names and identifying information (unless otherwise noted) have been changed to protect their privacy, but the words are theirs verbatim.

This book is not meant to be a research study. Instead, it is an anecdotal consideration of the experience of midlife adults who have gamely presented their most personal memories of growing up, their intimate recollections of the parents who raised them, and the issues and changes they have encountered since being orphaned. My interview questions were drawn from my personal experience. My journal, which I have kept since 1970, provided a resource for all the emotions that I experienced during the dark days as my parents were dying and in the aftermath. I was all too aware of how watching our parents face death affects our outlook on our mortality. We begin to think about our own death. We start to examine our relationships and to alter them accordingly. Reaching deep inside ourselves, we define who we are at this juncture. And while we may not always be able to identify the changes that we are undergoing, it is evident that the death of our last parent indisputably makes an impact on us.

As you listen to the voices of these midlife orphans, you will begin to see that much of your experience, while yours alone, is a predictable and reasonable reaction to the grievous loss of the last parent. We are indeed orphaned when our last parent dies and it takes time to adjust to our altered status from adult child to adult. In this new role, we are forced to step to the helm, where we can no longer deny death—or its antithesis, life and personal growth—that is the legacy of this rite of passage. Our only choice is to seize our legacy. *Midlife Orphan* is a chronicle of those who are doing just that.

THE RIDE

"C'm-o-n down!" shouts the announcer to a wildly enthusiastic audience. *Luanda, Elizabeth, and Richard bound down the aisle to compete in one of America's favorite game shows. It's time for "The Price Is Right."*

From my vantage point, I see only the glow of the screen. Sinking back into the luxurious, cushioned seat, I inhale the limousine's leathery odor. My fingers trace the stitching in the smoky gray upholstery.

My son Dan, at fourteen, is visibly uncomfortable in necktie, blazer, and pants that strain around his midriff. He slouches next to me. His younger brother, eleven, sits cross-legged on the floor, glued to the small TV, his white shirttail slipping out of his gray flannel pants.

Andy spotted the TV the minute we opened the limo door. "Hey, cool."

He attempted, unsuccessfully, to switch it on, then stood to tap on the glass partition.

"Chauffeur, could you turn on the television? Pul-lease?" he added beseechingly.

"No TV," reproached his aunt.

"Oh, let him watch it," I said, much less concerned with convention than my sister.

It's a slow, long ride to the funeral home. The day is dark and gloomy and a heavy rain falls. Traffic is crawling. The tension is palpable. Like the glass panel that separates us from the driver, another shield, this one invisible, stands between my sister and me. In it are reflected childhood wounds that have re-opened under the strain of the past four months. Despite our mutual sorrow, we haven't been able to comfort each other as we helplessly watched our mother's swift surrender to brain cancer.

The driver has obligingly turned on the small television set. Andy busies himself tuning it in.

"Turn the volume down," his aunt requests.

I study my child as he grudgingly complies. His head is tilted slightly, his tongue pushes his lip out over his upper teeth. The only sign of apprehension is his rapid blinking.

We are riding to his grandmother's funeral—my mother's funeral. Just sixteen months ago, we traveled this same route to bury my father. It is all too familiar.

The sound of Bob Barker's voice penetrates my numbness. He is calling for bids on a ballroom-sized crystal chandelier.

"What do you bid?" Andy pivots to look at his aunt.

Silence. And then . . .

"Fifteen hundred dollars," she allows, tentatively.

"Eighteen hundred," chimes in my brother-in-law.

My sister turns to her daughter.

"Eighteen seventy-five," says my niece, the chic young lawyer.

"You're too high," rebukes her brother, tossing his unruly shoulder-length mane. *"I say twelve hundred dollars."*

"What's your bid, Dan?" my now eager sister addresses my older son. It appears that she welcomes this distraction as much as I do.

"Sixteen hundred," replies Dan.

"Mom?" Andy gazes at me.

"Sixteen hundred and one," I answer, attempting to apply some strategy.

"And what about you, Andy?" His aunt looks at him expectantly.

"Two thousand," he replies in a flash.

I crane my neck to see the screen as the audience begins to hoot and holler. The winner is Luanda. She jumps up and down, screaming and blowing kisses at her boyfriend in the audience. Andy punches the air with his right fist and shouts "Yes!" His bid is only fifty dollars under the actual price. Everyone congratulates him.

We continue to play along with the studio audience, calling out our bids and laughing at the contestants' fervor. The tension, at least for now, has abated.

With uncanny timing, the program ends as we pull into the parking lot of the funeral home.

"That's it. And no TV when we ride to the cemetery," says my sister to my son, veiling herself in the cloak of propriety.

Andy clicks off the television.

My sister and her family slide along the seat and climb out of the limousine. My older son exits next. Andy hangs back, then grabs my hand and, gently, I push him out before me. We step into the chilly air. A mantle of large, black umbrellas, a courtesy of the funeral home, protects us from the downpour.

Andy pulls himself up straight and attempts to jam his shirt into his pants. His brother stands by my side, awkward despite the six inches he has over me.

"You okay, Mom?" Dan asks shyly.

Nodding wordlessly and swallowing to excise the tightening in my throat, I put my arms around my children, pulling them close.

I take a deep breath and then slowly exhale, struggling to contain the panic that is rising within me.

"*Let's go,*" I whisper to my sons.

It's time to mourn, *I add silently.*

Again.

ORPHANHOOD

On Becoming an Orphan

 $\mathcal{T}$ he call from the nursing home came in the middle of the night. The luminescent digits on my clock indelibly etched the time into my memory.

"I'm so sorry but your mother passed away a short while ago."

Did I want to come see her before the body was moved?

No, I don't want to leave the kids alone and, besides, the back roads to the nursing home are too icy, the aftermath of the blizzard of '93 that has blanketed the East Coast with three feet of snow.

After phoning my sister and brother-in-law, I remained in bed, unable to sleep, not wanting to wake my sons, too numb to cry or to call anyone. This was not the way I had envisioned the end, as if anyone could picture the moment at all. When the doctor told us several weeks before that her body was shutting down, I could not, would not imagine my mother's death. I had weeks to adjust to the idea of losing her, my last parent, but still I was not prepared for what I felt that night.

"I'm an orphan. I don't have any parents. I'm really an or-

phan." The thought whirled wildly through my gray matter, re-
peating like the words on one of my old records when the playing
needle caught in the grooves. I was forty-seven, the mother of
two boys, a writer with a modestly successful career. I had left
home at eighteen, bound for college hundreds of miles away.
After graduation, I'd moved to another city. I'd traveled across
the world alone. I had married, had two children, and divorced.
I hadn't lived with my parents in more than twenty-five years.
But on the night of my last parent's death, I longed for my father
and mother with a ferociousness I hadn't felt in decades. For forty-
seven years, I was their daughter. In the space of little more than
a year, I had become an orphan.

In the sobering hours that followed the death of my last parent,
I replayed the movie of my childhood. Once again, I was the ten-
year-old on the surgical table, wincing silently as the doctor ex-
tracted bone marrow from my hip. The nurse wiped the
perspiration from my forehead and urged me to squeeze her hand.
I wanted Mommy and Daddy. In the next frame, I was a high
school senior, shuttled to family friends the week of my graduation piano recital because Dad was undergoing life-threatening
surgery out of town. My boyfriend was in the enthusiastic audience that rewarded me with a standing ovation, but without my
parents there to *kvell* (this is the Yiddish term for expressing excessive pride), my triumph was not quite as sweet.

The night my last parent died, the anxiety, fear, and panic of
those early traumas (no matter how inadvertent) returned to haunt
me. Bathed in a pale wash of the clock's emerald glow and the
blanched moonbeams that peeked through the slats of the wooden
blinds, I was more the bereft child than the grieving adult.

Anticipating Orphanhood

Each of us knows that someday our parents must die. It's one of those facts of life that rests on the back burner where our parents' love simmers through the years like a rich soup stock. At what point do we confront the fact that the light under the pot will go out one day?

In reality, what has been referred to as "anticipatory grief" begins as soon as love is implanted.[4] We see it as separation anxiety, evident early in a child's life. Witness a nine-month-old baby cling to Mommy or Daddy when Grandpa, a favorite until now, tries to hold his grandchild. Observe the toddler who saunters away from his parents, gleefully independent. Suddenly, he stops to look back. Are they still there? Maybe he will run back to grab Daddy's leg before taking off again. We listen empathetically and reassure the child who verbalizes his fear that Mommy or Daddy might die like Aunt Anna did. As renowned child development specialist Dr. Haim G. Ginott wrote, "if death is a riddle to adults, to children it is an enigma veiled in mystery."[5]

Children are ingenious at expressing separation anxiety indirectly, as my sons did when their father and I split up. The boys were then five and eight and the separation turned their lives upside down. Inevitably, an off-the-scale tantrum over something seemingly trivial—the baked beans touching the hot dog or an inadequate proportion of chocolate syrup to milk—would be followed by a revelation of some fear or concern once things quieted down. Frequently, it was speculation about what would happen if their father or I died.

I understood that the tantrums were not because my children were spoiled or bratty. They were frightened. Their safe, secure world had been toppled. Their frustration, like their shirts that refused to stay tucked in, was poised to erupt at the slightest provocation. My younger son, whose extraordinary imagination fanned the fires of his insecurity, concocted scenarios in which his father and I died on the same day in separate accidents. With whom would he and his brother live? Would he be able to keep his room, his friends? The issue of separation and loss loomed large with unending questions and deep-seated fears, magnified in this case by his parents' estrangement but not so very different from the fears of most children as they begin to separate from their parents.

By adolescence, we understand (intellectually, at least) that in the natural order of events, our parents will die before us someday. But that's a long way off. At eighteen, we're invincible, and by default, so are our parents. We move away from home, confident that we won't return, but it's reassuring to know that the option is there.

As we become adults, we accept on a more conscious level that our parents aren't going to be around forever. We cannot avoid signs of their aging—their gait is slower, limbs tremor, and memories are failing. We grow older and so do they. Increasingly, we become their caretakers. We may move them to more comfortable or appropriate surroundings. We assist them in making end-of-life decisions, such as medical directives and living wills. Despite the guilt it invokes, we may even begin to think about our inheritance, especially if we are contributing to the cost of their care. In one way or another, we are preparing for their death.

Sidney and Miriam Moss, a husband-and-wife research team in Philadelphia who have been studying aging and death for two decades, explain there is less taboo in anticipating one's parent's death than the death of a spouse or a child.[6] Parental death may be the natural order but, though they may even have rehearsed their parents' death in their minds, most adult children are understandably reluctant to think about the end of their parents' lives. This became clear when scores of people I met, upon learning what I was writing about, told me they couldn't imagine being orphaned, that it was too upsetting to think about. Many adults said, "I have only one parent left. I can't face losing that one too." Very few expressed this thought to the surviving parent.

It's relatively easy to sit down with Mom and Dad to decide who will get the bone china someday and who gets the baby grand piano. It is much more difficult to say, "I can't imagine life without you. It saddens me and frightens me to think that someday you'll be gone and I won't have any parents anymore. I will miss you." And for most adult children, this sentiment is true.

Never the Right Time

In his excellent book *The Orphaned Adult,* Rabbi Marc Angel questions the reaction of adult children to their elderly parents' unexpected death, pointing out that their death, while not expected at the time, "could have been foreseen, at least theoretically."[7] Signs of aging and illness are warnings of impending death. One might expect that this awareness would prepare us for this event, lessening the grief.

Although there are few studies on the death of the last parent, a number of studies have looked at the degree of reaction in adults who have lost a parent and the circumstances of the death. Findings indicate that even when death terminates a prolonged illness and might be a welcome relief, the pain felt by adult children can be intense.[8]

Gina, a fifty-year-old homemaker and mother of two grown children, expresses the thoughts of many midlife adults when the last parent dies: "I just wasn't ready for it. You know, I have a friend whose husband was in the process of dying at the time when my mother died. This friend helped me understand that dying is as natural as living. I never used to view it like that. Now I see that we have to accept dying as part of God's plan. But I just wasn't ready for it when it happened."

Who is ever ready for death? Maybe the best we can do is to say "it's time" when a loved one's suffering is too painful to watch. This allows us to let go of the physical presence. Letting go emotionally is much more complicated.

My parents were not young when they died. In fact, they lived fairly long lives: my mother lived to the age of seventy-eight, my dad until he was eighty. But it wasn't long enough for me. Why couldn't they have lived even longer? Why couldn't my father, a civil engineer, live to see his grandson go off to college to pursue his own interest in engineering? Although computer engineering hadn't been an option for him, Dad would have enjoyed sharing his grandson's passion. As Dan put it when he got a state-of-the-art computer a couple of years ago, "Too bad Pop-pop couldn't have seen this. It would've been cool to teach him how to program. He'd think this computer stuff really rocks."

Indeed he would have. But unfortunately, several years before he died, Dan's grandfather was robbed of his sharp, analytic mind, his brain cells zapped by Alzheimer's disease. Like most family members of victims of this dreadful illness, I had grieved some while my father was alive but still I felt cheated by his unnatural death. Before the bus accident that ultimately killed him, he was physically healthy and his personality had remained remarkably intact. A favorite dance partner at his Alzheimer's daycare center, his affable sense of humor was still evident. He hugged the kids and me warmly when we visited. So what if he no longer remembered our names?

A year later, with chemotherapy wracking her body, my mother's will to live centered on my son Andy's Bar Mitzvah, only a year and a half away. She didn't make it. Why couldn't my parents have lived to see their youngest grandchild become a Bar Mitzvah? Why did their lives have to end before *I* was ready?

It is not unusual to hear adult children bemoan their parent's untimely death. My mother's death, no matter when it happened, would have been devastating, but to lose her so soon after my father's death seemed especially cruel.

"It's not fair," I whimpered to my friend Michael when I learned of my mother's inoperable brain tumor. "She's never been sick. I'm not ready for this. I can't remember ever seeing her sick."

"Would you feel any better if she *had* been?" he responded in his sardonic but gentle way.

I had to laugh, in spite of myself.

When Long Isn't Long Enough

George, a tall, gregarious professional singer, tells me about his eighty-year-old aunt who recently lost her mother, who was a hundred and two years old when she died. "My aunt says that as long as her mother was alive, she had that feeling that she was someone's child. All of a sudden, at eighty, she has to think completely for herself."

To be sure, George's aunt is at the extreme end of the spectrum and chances are, she had been doing her own thinking for a long time. Most of us don't have a parent by the time we reach our eighties, although with life expectancies rising, this scenario is likely to become more common. Nonetheless, his story illustrates that the attachment to our parents continues throughout life, no matter how long that may be. When we have trusted that genetics will keep our parents around for a long time, it can be particularly troubling, as it was for Ray, when a parent dies sooner than we expect.

Ray was thirty-seven when his mother died suddenly while recuperating from kidney surgery. Six years later, his brother, his only sibling, was killed in an automobile crash. Now forty-eight, a successful bioengineer, and the sole survivor of his nuclear family, Ray struggles with the death of his father just a few months ago. He always assumed that genetics would assure his father a life well into his nineties, so it was shocking for Ray to see his father become debilitated when he did.

"I had a distorted view of aging, based upon the way my father aged." Ray describes his father as robust well into his eighties and recalls the exact date when his father was hospitalized for the first time in his life. "He was very active and worked a lot. Until he hit eighty-five, there was nothing to constrain him from doing whatever he ever wanted to do—nothing. He was eighty-seven years old when he went into the hospital for the first time. It was on November eighth. He died at eighty-eight, aging at the end exponentially."

Ray had felt certain that his dad would live easily to be a hundred since *his* mother had lived to a hundred and one and there was longevity on both sides of the family. Now he ponders his mother's untimely death and regrets that he didn't have more input into decisions about her medical care. Ray's reaction to his last parent's death is not unusual. He is grieving deeply and sifting through a barrage of mixed emotions. Ray is sorry about some things he didn't do or say. He always figured there was plenty of time. Unfortunately, he was wrong.

For Ray, Gina, and other adults like myself, it doesn't matter how long our parents lived. At death, their lives haven't seemed long enough. All of the life cycle events that our parents will miss—the births, christenings, Bar and Bat Mitzvahs, confirmations, graduations, weddings—create emotional black holes for us, their children. Every joyous celebration will now have a taste of bittersweet when we remember parents who are not here to share in our happiness.

The New Reality

"Recognizing that you are now an orphan is one of the issues that is unique to the loss of the last parent," explains Dr. Dana Cable, professor of psychology at Hood College in Frederick, Maryland. "We tend to associate the word 'orphan' with children but the reality is that anyone who has no surviving parents is really an orphan. Suddenly, the adult is hit with the fact that he or she has a new role."

Because each of us has a unique experience with our parents, our responses to the last parent's death are widely disparate. Yet, there was one sentiment that all the midlife adults I interviewed experienced in common—an acute awareness of a change in status. The experience of Portia, a teacher in her mid-forties, illustrates this.

An only child and single mother since her child's infancy, Portia did not anticipate that she would be so affected by her last parent's death. The renewed presence of her father, who had been emotionally distant for most of her life, at times intruded on the world she constructed for herself and her daughter after her mother died. Portia was caught off guard when her father's death left her so bereaved.

"I was thirty when my mother died. We were incredibly close. When she died, I was pretty numb for a long time. I was also angry because my relationship with my father was never close and when my mother was dying, my father suddenly tried to begin a relationship with me. Over time, I became his caretaker. When he died a few years ago, I didn't experience the sense of loss that I had when my mother died. But his death confirmed how utterly alone I really was. I had to face it and I had to make peace with it. It's taken a long time. I'm in a good relationship now—we're living together—but I think I'll always see myself as alone."

Not everyone experiences the sense of isolation that Portia does. But midlife adults frequently do feel very much alone when the last parent dies, even when he or she has a supportive partner. That is because the loss propels us to a new reality that we can understand intellectually but for which there is no way to prepare emotionally. Whether or not one considers oneself orphaned, there is no denying the message borne by the last parent's death— not only are we no longer anyone's child, we are now the older generation.

The older generation. Those were Olga's precise words when her father died. Olga is a professional fundraiser, divorced and re-married with two grown children from her first marriage. She is petite, with silky smooth skin that belies her sixty-two years. She was a young mother herself when her parents bitterly ended their thirty-three-year marriage.

Recalls Olga, "Being an only child was always a powerful emotional reality for me. I felt lonely and desperately wanted a sibling. My mother died when I was thirty-two and my father died a few years later. At that point, wonderful things were happening professionally for me after some very difficult years. I had gotten divorced, finished graduate school, and moved to the West Coast. At the time my father died, I was planning a major project and was completely preoccupied with my work. So when I got the call from my stepmother that my father had died, I didn't react immediately. I remember vividly that when I hung up the phone, the first thing I thought was, 'Oh, my God, I'm an orphan. What do I do now?' Then, even more upsetting, I realized that there was nobody to call—my father was an only child, too. I knew that from that time on, I was in a totally different place in my life. I was the older generation now."

While the sense of being orphaned and the awareness of a new rank are not one and the same, it is clear that the two feelings collide. Of the fifty-two adult children I interviewed, all but three felt orphaned. Everyone, however, was aware of being in a different place after the death of the last parent. This realization emerged at different points for different people.

At first Jill, a textile artist and mother of a fourth-grader, didn't experience the sense of being orphaned when her last parent died. Her immediate focus was on grieving for her mother, with whom she was very close. It wasn't until later that Jill began to feel "cut off," as she puts it. "As time passed, I had this growing sense of loss, this strange feeling that there would be no more holidays for my son at grandma's, no older generation to look to for advice. Your mind plays funny tricks . . . you feel this loss even though you may not have actually experienced holidays at Mom and Dad's or visited very often. I think it's because your parents are your sense of continuity with your past. You realize you've lost that whole connection. You're cut off from your history."

Ernie, a fifty-three-year-old retired successful stock analyst, frames his reaction from another perspective. Of his mother's death six months earlier, Ernie says, "What hit me most was that now I was the patriarch. That may be the flip slide of feeling like an orphan. I realized that the family name stops here." He and his younger brother are the last males in their family. Ernie's twenty-three-year-old daughter is the only grandchild. More than likely, Ernie's daughter and her husband will have children one day. Although the family name may not carry on, the lineage will continue. When Ernie talks about the end of the family name, he is actually addressing his altered status from son to patriarch. It isn't something that he dwells on; nonetheless, he is acutely aware of this role, particularly in his dealings with his younger brother, who was always more dependent on their parents.

For Bess, a fifty-three-year-old divorced lawyer and an only child who is childless, her last parent's death marked her revised placement in her family's history. "In terms of being the last of my family, oh yeah. . . . I was going through my mother's things after she died and I opened one drawer and there were books from the funerals of my great-great-grandmother, my grand-mother, my grandfather, and then my father. You have this feeling like you don't belong anywhere. Like this is it, you're the end of the line."

Older generation. End of the line. Or as Emma, a social worker and avid biker, puts it, "I just feel like I'm next on the firing range." This new status is a legacy of the death of the last parent and it is, for many midlife adults, the outcome that is the hardest to digest. It will be months, possibly even years before we suc-cessfully integrate our new rank with our midlife goals and dreams.

"Orphan" Defined

"What I remember most about that first day at the orphanage," begins Jim in his soft, soothing voice, "is the sound of the nun's shoes on the marble floor. I followed her up the steps. Her shoes made this loud clicking sound. She didn't speak a word to me. I remember feeling so small, standing in the hallway and looking up at the vaulted ceiling. When she opened the double doors into the dormitory and I saw the rows of beds, I knew something awful was happening and there was no one to rescue me."

The dictionary defines an orphan as a child bereaved of parents, a child whose mother and father are dead. Yet, an orphanage is often a refuge for children whose parents have abandoned them for one reason or another. And what really defines an orphan, according to Jim, is the loneliness, the sense of abandonment, and the constant longing.

Jim and his brother, whose parents split up when Jim was an infant, ended up in an urban Catholic orphanage for boys after years of moving from one foster home to another. Their father wasn't able to pay child support so state law forbade him to see his children. John's mother was an alcoholic who couldn't properly care for her children. Jim was eight when he and his older brother were placed in the orphanage. Their two half-sisters went to live in an institution twenty miles away and the siblings rarely saw each other through the years.

Life in the orphanage was underscored by a sense of helplessness and despair. Physical needs were met—Jim and the other boys dressed in secondhand clothing, ate bland but filling meals, and resided within thick stone walls that protected them from the elements. But there was no one to comfort the smallest hurt, no one to offer a goodnight hug or kiss. Birthdays went unacknowledged, marked by neither a gift, cake, or even a card. Accommodation was the way to survive. Jim hasn't forgotten the nights he smothered his cries into a pillow—such emotional displays were frowned upon. For Jim, being an orphan meant growing up without emotional comfort and support, the sustenance that most children get from their parents on a daily basis.

Heidi and her older brother were more fortunate than Jim. Each had enjoyed a warm relationship with two supportive parents whom they now miss terribly. Heidi recalls, "My brother was visiting me and we were sitting in a bar, reminiscing about our parents. 'Oh, you're orphans,' the bartender said, overhearing our discussion. I remember looking at my brother and saying, 'What is she talking about?' That's when we really started to talk."

Heidi is married, a part-time librarian, and the mother of a ten-year-old daughter. Her father died of leukemia when Heidi was nineteen. When her mother passed away six years ago, Heidi was thirty-five, her daughter just a toddler.

"I certainly feel a big void since they are gone. My brother has expressed similar feelings. When my mother died, I remember thinking, 'What am I going to do now?' I was just feeling so lost and so was my brother. We each felt lonely and abandoned, all of the things orphans feel, but we never attached them to the word *orphan* until that bartender's comment."

Why Do I Feel Like an Orphan?

Miriam, forty-one and the mother of two young children, lives in the suburbs of a large midwestern city. She is a stay-at-home mom whose husband works two jobs, which leaves him little time for his family. An only child, Miriam is disappointed in her marriage and struggles with feelings of resentment and loneliness. She is distraught at the loss of her parents at a time when her life feels so shaky.

She says, "I just wasn't ready to lose the security and the strength I got from my parents. I feel like an orphan—it's a really strange feeling. I talk to my mom's sister all the time but she has five kids of her own and five grandchildren. If one of them calls when she's talking to me, she'll excuse herself so she can talk to them. I'm not used to that. I feel really alone."

Miriam accepts that her aunt puts her own children first but this reality underscores the loss of her own parents, for whom she was the center of attention. Miriam believes that she will never enjoy that status again and she mourns this loss.

In contrast to Miriam's unhappy marriage, Jean's marriage of twenty-five years is a source of great comfort to her, and her career as an art therapist is quite satisfying. Nonetheless, she echoes Miriam's words. We sit in the kitchen of the spacious, stone colonial home that she shares with her husband and their two children. Jean's gentle face is framed by soft dark waves tinged with gray. Her father died twenty years ago and it has been eleven years since her mother passed away.

Jean chooses her words thoughtfully. "There's an aloneness like you've never felt before when your last parent dies. These are the people who cared about you beyond anything you can imagine. It's just like the way you care about your own kids. Once your parents are gone, there's nobody else who will ever be there for you like that, not even your spouse. But then again, you know that your children will be there for their children in the same way. It's something that's unique about the relationship between parents and children."

What exactly is this quality—this unique aspect of the parent/child relationship—that Jean describes? Why is the attachment to our parents so different from the attachment to a husband or wife of thirty years or to a brother or sister whom we've known for forty years?

Of all the relationships we experience, our relationship with our parents is the first significant one. Our earliest and most treasured memories begin with our mother and father. As the decades roll by, we create intimate connections with others and accumulate volumes of additional recollections but all the while we are building on that first relationship. Our parents' values and their experiences are tightly bound into our life's tapestry, tangled with threads that we weave for ourselves as our individual character evolves. Like Konrad Lorenz's goslings, we are imprinted by our parents, following because they are there to lead us. Eventually we leave to establish our own lives, but as long as our parents are living, we are their children. We may function quite well as an adult but it is not until we lose the last parent that we discover just how close to the surface the child within has been lurking.

For John, a youthful-looking married man now in his late forties, his mother's death six years ago awakened childhood feelings that had long been buried. John was just twenty-one when his father was murdered (the victim of a holdup) but he recalls his anxiety way before then.

"As a kid, I always had this terrible fear that my parents would die," explains John. "Whenever I did something wrong, I was sure that God was going to punish me and take away my mother or my father. I don't know where this fear came from, I just know it was there. So when my dad was killed, I fell apart. I was a mess for a long time. When my mother died twenty years later, I couldn't accept her death. You never think these things will happen to you. I was the last person I thought could handle losing both parents. I didn't think I could get through it. I remember thinking that God couldn't have done this to me, that I felt like I needed my mother so much.

"Although I had my own family—I was married twenty years at that point and my kids were grown—I felt awful. There's just something there with your parents—I can't describe it. Even now, I listen to people talking to their parents and—it could be even the littlest thing, bragging about their kid's report card— well, it hurts that I can't do that. You know, my mother wasn't particularly helpful and I didn't lean on her but just knowing that she was there was important. Losing her felt like abandonment. It left such an emptiness."

Mourning Our Family of Origin

Emptiness, abandonment—these are the words I heard over and over. If we are independent adults with our own lives and our own families, why does the death of the last parent leave us feeling so empty? This is the question that I asked myself in the weeks following the death of my last parent.

After the Shiva, the seven-day mourning period that Jews observe, life returned to normal. Or so it seemed. I resumed my writing, frantically trying to catch up to meet my deadlines. I sent out thank-you notes and cleaned my house. It appeared that I was fine, so everyone assumed that I was "back to normal." In truth, I wasn't fine at all. I was not sleeping well. I was feeling anxious, terribly lonely, and I was constantly weepy. Would I feel differently, I wondered, if I were married or had a significant other? Had I been more dependent upon my parents than I'd believed?

My kids, discomfited by my tears that spilled without warning, smothered me with hugs, reminding me, "You have us, Mom." I, in turn, assured them that they occupied nothing less than the penthouse of my heart. I explained that I was very sad, that I missed my parents, that my sadness would diminish in time, and, no matter what, I would always be here for them (thankfully, they never picked up on the irony of the latter). I said all the "right" things but I wondered whether this profound sorrow was going to permit me to grieve and to parent simultaneously.

Months after my mother's death, my grief was still so intense that I began to worry that something was wrong with me. This concern was exacerbated when I ran into a man I knew whose mother, a vital, active woman, had died of a heart attack two weeks before. I offered my condolences and, almost cheerfully, he commented on her good fortune to die quickly and painlessly. How could he be so cavalier? What was wrong with me?

I sought the help of the gifted therapist who had counseled me in the difficult years before and after my divorce. She helped me to understand that the loss of my last parent could not be an isolated bereavement. In this respect, the death of the last parent is a unique loss. We mourn not only that parent's death or the loss of both parents but something else as well. We are grieving for our family of origin—the last attachment to our childhood.

Losing the Past

Despite the depth of our relationships with spouse, significant other, children, siblings, and friends, the loss of our parents in midlife leaves us feeling as though something has been suddenly yanked from us. The adults I interviewed struggled to define what that "something" is. Had we lost a spouse or a child, the tempo of life would have changed dramatically. But when our last parent dies, the rhythm stays the same. We continue to sleep next to our spouse and sit at the dinner table with our children. We go to the same job, get together with friends, yet something, inexplicably, has changed. The only thing we know for sure is that we have landed in a different place.

John DeBerry, bereavement coordinator of the Northwestern Memorial Hospice Program in Chicago, explains, "When we lose a child, we lose our future. When we lose a peer, we lose the present, but when we lose our parents, we lose our past."

Minus my parents, I have little reason to visit Wilmington, Delaware, the town where I was born and raised. There is no longer a conduit to the steady diet of news about former school chums. So it was nearly two years after the fact that I learned of the death of the father of a high school friend with whom I keep in touch only sporadically. When I do go to Wilmington, it is to visit friends who settled there during my last summer at home. They don't know the people I grew up with, most of whom have moved away. On occasion, I drive by the homes in which I spent so much time and I wonder what happened to Bruce and Carol and Allen and if they still have their parents. I have no way of knowing. It is less than thirty miles from where I live but my hometown is now a lifetime away.

While working on this book, I call my aunt (my mother's lone surviving sibling) to ask the year that my parents were married. She recalls that she was about twelve or thirteen at their wedding and we calculate the date to 1936. As we chat, she remarks how disconnected she feels at times, how she misses her parents and her older sisters. And without those sources, her knowledge of the family's past is limited. Though I am twenty-two years younger, I understand completely. With my last parent's death, a significant link between my past and my present has been severed. What is left is a void in which my unanswered questions float. The one source that had preserved my childhood no longer exists. It's a discomforting feeling.

Ronni, a crafts boutique owner, concurs. "With my parents gone, I feel like I've lost touch with my family history. There's no one to tell me stories about the past. I haven't had grandparents in a while so there's really a loss of generations. I've got six siblings. My parents were at the hub, the reason we all gathered together. Now we're trying to reassemble our family, but the truth is that some of us are more interested in creating a bond than others."

Ronni's brother Chris expresses a similar sense of loss. He wishes he had asked his parents more questions about who they were and where they came from. "We heard some stories, mostly from my mother, not many from my father. I wish I knew more about what my father was like when he was growing up."

Chris and Ronni acknowledge mutual sadness over the loss of the family home in New England, the setting of so many idyllic summers. Without the house, they and their five siblings, who have spread their wings from Maine to Colorado, had no single place to gather when they returned to the area to release their father's ashes in the cove he loved.

For those adults whose parents were still living in the family home at their death, its loss is particularly acute, compounding the loneliness of losing the last parent. Jay, a marketing consultant from Wisconsin, describes his return to his hometown with his siblings when their father died.

"The night my father died, I was in Montreal. My sister called with the news and I told her I'd take a plane 'home' that night. When my wife asked where we were all going to stay, I realized I didn't have a clue. My dad had moved out to their small lakeside cottage after my stepmother died, so we no longer had the family home. You assume your home is always going to be there. I called my sister back and I asked, 'Where the heck are we going to stay?' We picked a small lodge that had about eight rooms where all of us as a family could be together. So we stayed there."

For George, a trip "home" to tie up loose ends left him feeling particularly melancholy and alone. He explains, "Your parents are gone in body, not in spirit, but you feel kind of disconnected from your ancestry. I didn't feel it until my father died because when mother died, we still had him. But with both of them gone, it's pretty weird. There's no one in our house. When I went down to take care of some legal matters and final details, there was no one there. The house was empty. It was a really odd feeling. That's the first time I felt like an orphan."

Confronting Our Mortality

Studies on midlife suggest that it is a significant turning point in human development. Carl Jung, one of the first psychologists to look at the middle years, concluded that our main task in the second half of life is to refocus our life around a new set of values. In contrast to the more materialistic, extroverted values of earlier years, these are values that are spiritual in nature.[9] The death of parents typically occurs in our middle years, just as we are beginning this inner search to understand the meaning of our own lives. The death of our last parent moves us even further on this path of emotional growth.

"I think we don't actually think of ourselves as adults until our parents die," says George. "As long as there's one parent still alive, I can still be the child. But when both parents are gone, it's like, 'Shit, I have to do this myself.' It's very unnerving.

"As long as you have a parent, even if that parent is ninety and you are seventy, you're still someone's child. It's shocking to lose your last parent because then you really don't have anyone."

But George, like most of the adult orphans that I interviewed, does have someone. He has a wife and children whom he clearly loves. Like George, most of us have formed intimate relationships by the time we are adults—with siblings, spouse, children, or close friends. Yet we feel so alone when our last parent dies. Perhaps it is not so much that we don't have "anyone" anymore. What is now missing is the shield between death and us. Minus that buffer, we are left to face our own mortality. It's an enormous blow, one that Donna, fifty-five, addresses head on.

"When my mother died, my older sister said, 'I feel like I have nothing behind me,' " explains Donna, who, at fifty-five, is a beautiful actress with a mane of lustrous black hair that she tosses dramatically. As she speaks, her hands flutter, punctuating sentences that roll out faster than coins from a change machine.

"My sister will continue to be the buffer between me and death if things go according to plan, although life never seems to. She's still very youthful but when she's not wearing any makeup and she pulls her hair back and takes her glasses off, she looks so much like my mother—so old—that I hate to see it. Then I have to think about what happens when she goes." She shudders. " I don't like to think about it."

For Donna, divorced in midlife, feeling attractive is important to her sense of well-being. When her mother finally died, Donna, who had prayed that her mother wouldn't suffer, was far from relieved. Was it because of that small voice inside of us that admits to not being quite ready to be totally adult? After all, the longer our parents live, the longer we can thwart our own aging.

"Having lost my parents, I think that mortality is right up there as an issue for me. I think about it a lot. I'm feeling quite old right now. I'm not as fit as I used to be because I changed from a physically active career to one where I'm much more sedentary. I'm very aware of aging and I'm afraid of dying," admits Ronni, who at forty-two is perfectly healthy, despite her concern about her fitness. "I think it's just going to intensify, this fear of aging, especially because I'm thinking about childbearing. We've been trying to get pregnant for four years and we're talking about adopting now."

For Ronni, confronting her own mortality is especially painful. A complex mix of emotions is driving her search to find a way to balance her fear of death with her desire to begin life. The issue of whether or not to have a child in midlife is not uncommon these days, but in Ronni's case, it has become an internal struggle intensified by her last parent's death. Confronting our mortality is a task of midlife but one that many adults choose to ignore.

Clearly, when the last parent dies, this denial is no longer possible. Brian, who describes himself as a bottom-line man, looked mortality in the eye when he celebrated a birthday after his father's death at age ninety-four.

"On my forty-seventh birthday, I realized I'd never be half my father's age again. It's a silly thing but I'm a numbers guy. The probability of me living to one hundred, well, it's not there. To the extent that I'm a deadline-oriented person, it's like, 'okay, you've got a deadline now.' " Brian laughs but it has a hollow ring and his eyes are mirthless.

Death is one deadline that no one is anxious to meet. Yet, it is when we have a deadline that we often accomplish the most. It's what nudges us on, pushing us to explore and to experiment while we have the opportunity. In the face of the deadline brought to our attention by our last parent's death, we find ourselves turning outward with renewed purpose and vigor. After all, there is much to do and no time to waste.

Eulogy, November 4, 1991

Dear Dad,

   We say goodbye to you with tremendous sadness and a measure of relief that this suffering has ended. You leave us, as all do, in body only. What remains is a legacy of love and cherished memories.

   Over the past two months, friends have asked if I was close to you. Sifting through the past for a response, I weighed each memory, trying to tip the scale to the side of close. Did I confide in you? Hardly ever. Did I ask your advice? Rarely.

   Were we close? You were the one who taught me to ride my two-wheeler in the block-long driveway behind our house. You ran alongside, letting go at precisely the right moment. You were the one who made grocery shopping an adventure—showing us how to spot the opened packages of candy and cookies, assuring us that it was okay to sample as long as the packages were already open. It was this one deviation from your usual high moral standards that made each cookie so wickedly delicious.

   Were we close? Once when I was about twelve, I breezed through the living room where you were watching a baseball game on TV. I remember saying, "I'll bet you're sorry you didn't have boys." You turned, as if struck, and answered, "I've never regretted it. I *love having daughters." I wasn't really worried but I never forgot those words.*

Were we close? When I was in college, you wrote to me regularly—funny, wonderful letters written in your broad, curlicued script, letters filled with lively anecdotes and colorful details that made me laugh. I was the only one of my friends to get letters from my father.

When I got my first real job and my own apartment, you took me aside to administer your fatherly advice— "Be careful with credit cards and pay off your bills each month." No preaching, just sensible straight talk. That was your style.

Were we close? When I became a mother and I couldn't stop Dan's cries, I handed him to you, assured that you would pacify him with your gentle rocking and crooning. You, whose lion's roar could terrify us when we were kids, were the gentlest of lambs when it came to babies. There wasn't a child in our family who hadn't been rocked to sleep by your soft singing.

Were we close? Just a few weeks ago, as I stood by your bedside crying, for a brief instant, you, barely conscious and connected to machines and restricted by the tube in your esophagus, directed your gaze to me and mouthed the words, "What's the matter?" Perhaps I imagined it. I don't think so but if I did, it reflects how I felt your concern always.

Were we close? You were my father, I was your daughter. In a more perfect world, we might have been closer. We might have known each other better. But in the world that is, we fashioned our relationship the only way we knew. You taught me not by word but by example. You were my father. You instilled in me your values of honesty and integrity. I love you for who you were and who you wanted me to be.

Were we close? You were my father. I, your daughter. Close enough.

GRIEF AND LOSS REEXAMINED

"What the soul needs, it uses. It is amazing how practically wise it can be about misfortune and accidents."

—JAMES HILLMAN, *The Soul's Code*

*W*hen my father died, I kept my sorrow as carefully contained as the freshly ground coffee I store in an airtight jar. Publicly, I expressed my feelings in a letter to my father, which I asked my friend Joyce to read at the funeral, lest I lose my composure. Privately, I allowed myself tears at intervals timed like my computer's backup, in short blips that assured me a safety valve but wouldn't distract me too much from my work. A painful divorce had put me on familiar terms with grieving and I wasn't too anxious to do it again.

Much has been written about grieving and loss. In the late sixties, Elisabeth Kübler-Ross forged the way for a public forum on death and loss with her extensive writings. Although others have studied grief, describing it in medical and psychological terms, it is Kübler-Ross's five stages of grieving—shock and denial, anger, bargaining, depression, and acceptance—with which we are most familiar. For too long, death had been a taboo subject. That is no longer true.

Today we have books, audiotapes, videos, support groups, and even Web sites to turn to for help. The week that I am writing this, National Public Radio's popular program *All Things Considered* has launched a series called "The End of Life." Models for dying and guides to grieving tell us that we can die with dignity and heal our grieving selves gently. Anne Hunsaker Hawkins wrote that ours is a culture in search of an *ars moriendi,* a model for "the good death." If death was taboo for earlier generations, "for us, it is bordering on an obsession."[10]

It is far easier to know grief than it is to comprehend what a good death might be. So public in its advent and private in its endurance, grief has often been compared to the cycle of the seasons. But to me, grief is more like the weather itself—unpredictably showering us just when we were certain that the rain had passed. That's grief—as persistent as an Indian summer and then, surreptitiously, like the purple crocuses that are so quickly replaced by a blaze of yellow daffodils that we scarcely notice their absence, it steals away. A tranquil hour becomes two or three. One productive day follows another. The mind starts to quiet. The heart is on the mend.

In the preface to his book *Understanding Grief: Helping Yourself Heal,* Dr. Alan D. Wolfelt offers that "grief is not something we as human beings 'get over.' Instead, it is something we live with." Anyone who has suffered a loss understands this at a gut level. We don't grieve one day and then put it away under lock and key. As thinking, feeling, ever evolving human beings, we are subject to shifting emotions as we grow and our circumstances change. What made us cry weeks after a loss may not elicit the same feeling a year later. Instead, we may find ourselves weeping over something entirely new, as Bess did.

Two months after her mother died, Bess was still having trouble getting out of bed each Saturday morning, the day that she had always spent shopping and lunching with her mother. She began to worry that she would never enjoy weekends again. One year later, she found herself in a wonderful relationship. Now she eagerly arose each Saturday, anxious to get chores done so she could spend the rest of the weekend with her boyfriend. As the relationship progressed, Bess began to experience intense sad feelings that confused her. Eventually, she realized that her despondency was because she could not share her newfound joy with her parents. For Bess, grieving will continue as she adjusts to a life without the parents with whom she was so close.

There is no walking away from grief. It pursues us relentlessly and, as psychologist and author Thomas R. Golden points out, the only way to deal with grief is to let it happen. Allie, whose father's death preceded her husband's by three months, concurs. "I have tried hard to pay attention to my grief and to let myself go through it in whatever way I had to. I just had to walk through it."

I wonder sometimes whether the current emphasis on how we die and how we grieve does us a disservice. What is a good death and whom does it benefit? The dying or the survivors? For a long time, I couldn't admit how angry I was that my mother had been so terrified of dying. Her anguished cries to me, "Don't let me die," filled me with rage and frustration, leaving me feeling so helpless. I wanted her to accept dying like a movie heroine. But my mother was no heroine, she was simply human. I have had to learn to accept that.

If our loved one suffers at the end, how does that affect us, the survivors? The truth is, death is rarely beautiful. In our society, more often than not, death means tubes, machines, or, at the very least, painkillers that anesthetize not only the pain but also the personality. Who's to say whether it is more merciful to prolong dying or to eliminate these? Will a "good death" make our griev-ing easier?

Because I did not set out to quantify grief, I cannot answer these questions definitively. But the adults I interviewed did not appear to have an easier time when the last parent had a "good death." Seth and his sister Lani found their mother's courage, openness, and good humor as she was dying inspirational. In sep-arate interviews, each detailed her spirit and determination. Her dedication to a good death may have helped her face her death with grace, but it did not mitigate her children's grief. A year after her death, these adult children were still grieving profoundly for their mother—for both their parents, whose alcoholism had marked their lives indelibly. Chris and his siblings are doing the same, struggling with issues that surfaced when their father died, despite a death that he faced courageously.

If you study the stages of grieving, you'll learn that the anger you feel right now over your father's death is temporary and in time you'll reach acceptance. Is it helpful to know that? This is a life lesson we learn after we've lived through loss and can appre-ciate the nuances of grief. Perhaps all we really need to know is that grief, with all its stages, is a natural process. Here, I deliber-ately use the word *natural* rather than *normal*. If we label something "normal" and we deviate from this standard, it's easy to conclude that anything otherwise is abnormal. Much research has been con-ducted on grieving and loss. Many professionals equate intense grief reactions with illness and believe that such grieving requires clinical attention.[11] And that may indeed be so. If you assume that grief is something you "get over," then these responses make sense. But grief is so personal, so curiously individual, that I am wary of diagnoses that may fail to acknowledge that as unique as each of us is, so too is our grieving experience.

Susan Balis, M.S.S., a therapist with a private practice in Philadelphia, looks at grief therapy through the eyes of the midlife orphan that she is. "I don't agree with specializing in something like grief because grief is a normal part of human life. I'm always worried about therapists who want to take people through specific stages at specific times because if you get into that, you're losing the complexity of how people function. I mourned my father differently than I mourned my mother, and it had to do with what those relationships were. If you're a fairly good general therapist, you can usually help people with their grief."

Perhaps it's more productive, instead of noting our progress by where we are in the various stages of grief, to recognize that there are those who hardly shed a tear when a loved one dies while some wail or shout. Others find themselves weeping for weeks or months. Some persons seem to have excessive energy following a profound loss while others can barely get out of bed. There are adults who seem fine initially after a loss but later develop physical ailments. Some individuals want only to get away. Others cocoon.

Not only is how we grieve variable, often we don't even know we are grieving. When Herb, a sixty-two-year-old accountant, says of his reaction to his last parent's death, "I haven't shed one goddamn tear," he assumes he hasn't grieved. Upon questioning, Herb clarifies that in his family, between males, a handshake was considered a show of affection. Herb says his reaction disturbs him and that he is working on his inability to express his emotion in his men's group. In the meantime, he is putting enormous energy into his role as executor of his father's estate. In fact, Herb *is* grieving, but his grief is not as obvious as if he were crying or acting depressed. Herb's way of grieving is not uncommon for a man, especially upon the death of the last parent.

Psychologist Tom Golden explains that for a man, "the death of the last parent often leaves him with a great sense of responsibility. Grief will manifest itself in those efforts that honor the family and hold the family together." This is precisely what Herb is doing—working feverishly to settle his parents' sizeable estate and to keep the peace between his many siblings, who have multiple opinions about the way the estate should be divided.

Undoubtedly, it is comforting to realize that everyone grieves in his or her own way, according to the cycles of self, rather than the cycles of grief. This is what Allie discovered as she found her way through the darkest time of her life. Two years after losing her father and husband, Allie lost her mother to cancer. After her mother's death, Allie was understandably emotionally spent. She quit a job that had become unbearably draining and traveled for six months, staying with friends. She found herself thinking about death a lot. She began to study how other cultures looked at death and dying, visiting an ashram for several weeks. Allie spent time sailing, a sport she and her husband had loved. On her own for the first time, she tried racing, something they had not done together. She found it exhilarating.

It's been two years since her mother died and Allie feels that she hasn't fully grieved her last parent's death. But in the lengthy course of her grieving, she has reconstituted her life by changing careers and solidifying friendships. She says, "The feeling now is one of freedom. I wake up in the morning and I'm no longer in pain. I'm really happy inside myself. I'm becoming the person I always wanted to be. I think I'm a better person from all of this tragedy. I look at the people who look like they're sailing through life and I think that they're also not in life, that they haven't touched it. It's not like suffering does it for you, but without it, you just don't really know about life."

If we turn our gaze inward to pay attention to how we are grieving and to integrate that with our sense of self, as Allie did, we can learn much about ourselves. Just as grief encompasses us, it also liberates us. Having lived through loss, we are stronger and more compassionate. We don't "get over" losing someone we love but it is one of life's blessings that the loss of a loved one does not diminish our capacity to find love or happiness once again.

Capacity for Grief

When my sons were young, we lit Sabbath candles each Friday night. One night, just before we were to say the blessing, the boys engaged in a fierce competition for my attention. To defuse the battle, I recited a story I'd read in a magazine in the pediatrician's waiting room earlier that day. The author, an expectant mother, had used the analogy of Sabbath candles to teach her children about the capacity for loving their soon-to-be new sibling.

Lighting the first candle with a match, she explained to her children that the flame represents all the love she has for them. Then she used the candle's flame to kindle the other candle. As it ignited, she noted that the second flame is the love for the unborn baby. She pointed out that even though the first candle used its flame to light the second one, its flame was not diminished.

I think often about that story. It seems that its lesson about love applies as well to loss. Just as our capacity for love grows exponentially, so does our capacity for grief. We don't mourn our last parent less because we have already mourned for the first one.

The loss of the first and probably longest-running relationship we have known takes a weighty toll. Gone is our family of origin. If our experience has been positive, we are distraught at the termination of this part of our life. If our relationship was troubled or our memories are not especially fond ones, along with the last parent's death goes any hope of changing things for the better.

And when our last parent dies, we lose the buffer that has shielded us from our own death, leaving us face-to-face with our mortality. Why shouldn't we grieve loud and long?

Disenfranchised Death

"Every day I go walking with my girlfriend who lives just across the street," begins Sheila, a physical therapist. "I was telling her that I was going to be interviewed for this book about midlife orphans and she laughed. She thought I was joking. She said to me, 'Of all the things that you've done in your life, you're being interviewed because your parents died? That's easy.' She thought it was funny. She just couldn't understand how important it was to me. She has one parent left who lives with her now. But until it happens to you, until you don't have any parents, I don't think you can understand the impact."

Sheila comments that her friend is not insensitive but rather like most of her coworkers. When Sheila talked about feeling like an orphan at the community hospital where she works, the response she got was mostly quiet stares. "These are my friends, the people I work with every day. They thought I was nuts."

Sheila's words echo those I heard from midlife orphans repeatedly—that friends and coworkers do not comprehend or appreciate the magnitude of the loss of the last parent. The loss of a parent simply does not elicit the kind of empathy that other losses do. It's not that people aren't sympathetic, but had we lost a child, a sibling, or a spouse, our grief, however prolonged or protracted, would be more acceptable. When we don't get "back to normal" within a few weeks after the death of the last parent, we are suspect. Perhaps we were too attached to Mom or Dad.

Maybe we were dependent or emotionally unstable. What else explains the prolonged mourning?

Psychologist Dr. Dana Cable calls the reaction to the death of the last parent a "disenfranchised" grief. "We assume you don't grieve long after the death of a parent. So, many adult orphans have a difficult time because they are not finding the societal support that there would be if a spouse, for example, had died."

Jill, an attorney, mother, and midlife orphan, agrees that this society denies death and doesn't allow people to do their grieving. She felt pressure to "get on with it" and get back to normal after her last parent died. It has changed Jill's awareness. She comments, "I've become much more conscious of that and now I'm more sensitive to the needs of grieving people."

With the trend away from rituals and social customs in this century, notes German sociologist Dr. Martin Doehlemann, there is a "silent" sadness or mourning when we lose a loved one.[12] After the last parent dies and the public mourning ends, adult orphans tend to turn inward to deal with this unique loss. We find ourselves mourning privately, reflecting on our parents and our childhood but keeping our feelings and thoughts largely to ourselves.

Lani, whose mother's death followed her father's by four years, coped with her grief largely with the support of her housemate, a widow, rather than her siblings. She says, "In the beginning, people asked how I was doing. Pretty soon, nobody asked anymore. Unless you've experienced the death of someone close to you, you don't ask how someone's doing after they lose a loved one, you assume they're doing okay. It's like living in your own world when someone dies. No one's really a part of it. Even my brothers and sisters, we talk to one another and someone will call on the holidays and ask if I'm okay and I say, 'Yeah, you know I miss Mom and Dad,' but that's about all we say about it."

The Prologue to Grief

A few nights after my mother's brain biopsy, I dream that my mother and I are playing Scrabble. I choose my letters and place them on the wooden holder. I shuffle my squares around to form a word but I freeze when I see what word my letters spell—D-E-A-T-H-L-Y. Mom is getting impatient waiting for me to take my turn. I can't move. Finally, I pass and toss in my letters.

The next night I dream that I am in a darkened room with my head locked in a steel vise. A doctor is drilling into my skull—I'm having a brain biopsy. The pressure is unbearable and I wake up crying and clutching my hair.

The following night I dream again, this time in vivid Technicolor. Bombs are cascading from an indigo sky, trailing ribbons of brilliant white light. I'm searching frantically for my children. I find Andy and yell to him to get into the basement while I search for his brother. Then I am running with Dan, pushing him down to shield him with my body as we run. I wake up panting. My mother is dying and I have begun to grieve.

Throughout our lives, we grieve for all kinds of losses, not just for the dead. In his book *Swallowed by a Snake: The Gift of the Masculine Side of Healing,* psychotherapist Thomas R. Golden relates grief to desire. "If your desire is met, you may find joy, and if it isn't, there is grief." Golden writes that there is no formula that can predict a person's emotional response to losing his or her desire. He contends that the so-called five stages of grief—denial, anger, sadness, bargaining, and acceptance—are experiences that have no particular order. Grief is with us throughout the process of watching a loved one die, not just after death, and we shift back and forth from one emotion to another throughout the process.

Many adult children care for ailing parents for a number of

years. When our parents are sick or terminally ill, we often begin grieving for them before their death, although we don't always realize it. Like many relatives of Alzheimer's patients, our family began to grieve, albeit subconsciously, when Dad's illness was diagnosed. My grief was masked by so many other emotions that it wasn't clear even to myself that I was in mourning. It was not unlike the years prior to my divorce when I didn't understand that underscoring all the anger and hurt was abundant sadness. I was grieving my failing marriage long before it was over. But divorce, which is so often compared to death, is strikingly different in one respect—we can find another partner or fashion another marriage but we can never replace parents. When our last parent dies, that primary relationship is gone forever.

When we watch a loved one die, it is normal to hang on to whatever essence is left for as long as we can, as I did as my father's disease progressed. Each visit left me whirling in a huge cauldron of emotion—relief that his body remained healthy, anger at the disease that was robbing him of his mind, longing for the father I had once known, and guilt for wishing for an end. At my father's funeral, my mother asked the rabbi to recite a poem from a newsletter of her local Alzheimer's Association, reprinted from a newsletter of the Lincoln, Nebraska, chapter. It is unfortunate that the author remains unknown because it is a haunting poem, capturing the lengthy grieving process that accompanies this tragic illness. I include it here because it speaks to anyone who watches a loved one die.

It's a Long Goodbye

She's leaving me, little by little, I wish she wouldn't go.
I will be there, as long as she needs me. How do I let her know?

I'd like to hold on to the memories, I'd also like to share.
But she's further away, getting further away. And yet, she's always there.

It's a long goodbye, and yet I believe that she can sense us.
So much time between now and then, when it's time against us.
There are times she almost seems like herself.
Sometimes it's just a phase. A part of the person I once knew,
and sometimes just a trace.

It's a long goodbye and still I don't know just what to say.
There's so much time between now and then,
because she goes away, a long goodbye.
Tell me how do all the others do it? There's so much time
between now and then.
How do we get through it? It's a long goodbye.

Not only do adult children grieve when a parent is terminally ill, but we also deal with the other parent's reaction, which can become tremendously burdensome and compound our own grief. Jim, a fifty-three-year-old consultant, recalls his distress at his father's decline when his mother got sick. "My mother lost her speech entirely in her last year. It was frustrating for both of my parents. They had always been so happy together. Dad was always very strong and stern throughout my entire life. But that last year, he was like a lost puppy. What was most shocking was to see how Dad sort of dissolved after she died."

Adult children frequently say that their grieving started at the point when the last parent's health began to deteriorate. Until that point, the existence of the surviving parent, regardless of his or her condition, provides a measure of security and comfort. The existence of a remaining parent cushions us from the reality of impending orphanhood. When the last parent begins to deteriorate, the advent of orphanhood can no longer be avoided.

Researchers who have studied grief reactions looked at the issue of the impact of death from a lengthy illness versus that of sudden death. When parents have been ill for a long time, is death a relief and is grieving easier? Or is a sudden death for an elderly person easier for the adult child who has not had to watch that parent suffer? Lani, who has experienced the loss of both parents, says, "What's better in terms of losing your parents? Losing them quickly or having time to prepare? It all comes out even in the end. It's just that when you have time to prepare, you start grieving the minute you find out that the person is sick."

Interestingly, in a 1981 study that looked at the reaction of adult children to their parent's death, researchers found no difference in the impact of sudden death and a gradual death on the child's way of coping.[13] In my interviews, I found that how we grieve is not so much a result of what kind of death our parents experienced as much as it is about our own emotional makeup.

Goodbye Again

When my father died, I mourned his death on fast forward. Who had time? My mother, exhausted from years of caring for Dad, was like my withered perennial garden after the harsh winter, desperately in need of tending. In the months after my father's death, my sister Candy, and I continued to run back and forth to my mother's apartment, three-quarters of an hour away. Mom had an insatiable need for our company. Formerly she had prided herself on her self-reliance, but after my father died, her energy level was sapped. She complained of headaches and exhaustion. This was not the mother I knew.

Alternating between empathy, guilt, and impatience, I attempted to tend to my mother, parent my children, and keep my career afloat. I resented her constant requests for my company and assistance with routine chores and her obvious distress when I wouldn't comply. She had never learned to drive, relying instead on my father. "Find a driver, Mom," Candy and I encouraged. There were legal issues to settle and bills to be paid. We had to sort through my father's belongings and straighten out finances. The apartment had grown shabby and was in need of repairs— Dad had unwittingly done lots of damage, breaking locks, destroying furniture, and ruining upholstery. At home, there were the usual daily minutiae to worry about. There was barely time for a life and clearly no time to mourn. And so, it wasn't until my mother died that my real grieving began.

With each death that we experience, we learn that no bereavement is isolated. Many years ago, when my younger son was in third grade, he witnessed a terrible tragedy—a plane and a helicopter crashed over his school playground. The crash made national news because Senator John Heinz was killed, as were two little girls who were playing that day in the April sunshine. With hundreds of other parents, I attended a meeting with a local psychologist. He explained that each child would deal differently with the tragedy, depending upon his or her history of loss.

Within each of us, there grows a compendium of loss. Each death evokes renewed grieving for previous losses. The death of the last parent, in particular, often reactivates mourning for the first parent. As adult children, many of us do not fully mourn the first parent because we become so preoccupied with the surviving parent. Thus, the second parent's death plunges us into what can feel like a bottomless pit of emotion as we struggle with grief that had not previously been fully acknowledged.

Initially, we may not recognize what is happening. We may be exhausted by the time our last parent dies. We attribute this tiredness to the stress of the events surrounding the death and, indeed, it is due to that. We have been running back and forth to the hospital. Some people have been making long distance trips for months. We may feel "out of sorts," tired, lethargic, bored, or depressed. But as weeks pass, we begin to question the depth of our sorrow. Many adults have vivid dreams about the parent who died first, no matter how many years ago. We wonder why we feel so lousy and why this pervasive sadness is lingering for so long.

The months after my mother's death were spent cleaning out my parents' apartment. We sorted through boxes of canceled checks, pay stubs dating back to the 1940s, and correspondence from their newlywed days. Weeks later, when I was just beginning to regain my equilibrium, I was sifting through one of the cartons that I had stored in my basement, looking for my mother's birth certificate. What I found tossed me into a renewed fit of mourning that I actually dubbed "mourning, round three."

On a sheet of graph paper imprinted with his company's logo, my father had copied a poem (author unknown), presumably with the Waterman fountain pen that he carried in his pocket protector, next to the ubiquitous mechanical pencil. It was a mushy, sentimental verse about the joy of having little girls, ending with the words, "Yes, she is a nerve-racking nuisance, just a noisy bundle of mischief. But when your dreams tumble down and the world is a mess, when it seems you are pretty much of a fool after all, she can make you a king when she climbs on your knee and whispers, 'I love you best of all!' "

This most tangible evidence of my father's love unleashed the storm that had been brewing within me. There was no more avoiding the pain of losing the father who taught me how to ride a two-wheeler, to make the bed with neat hospital corners, and to split open a fresh coconut. It was months after my mother's death, but memories of my father, now dredged up, began to poke at me at inopportune moments.

In the middle of conducting an interview for a feature about an engineering faculty member at a local university, an image of my father disrupted my line of questioning. The professor, a classical guitarist, was talking about his musical interest. As we chatted, I had a flash of Dad in the pirate costume he donned each Halloween, salvaged from his engineering school production of *The Pirates of Penzance*. I finished the interview with a lump in my throat and then ran to my car to have a good cry.

It's not always obvious which parent we are mourning when the last parent dies. For example, it is likely that Lani, a pediatric nurse in her thirties and one of nine children, is just beginning to acknowledge the impact of the loss of her father four years ago, although ostensibly she is mourning her mother's death last year. Lani and her siblings have disparate memories of their home life, but all remember the havoc that their parents' alcoholism created in the family. Her parents' drinking got so out of hand that when she was sixteen, a family intervention removed Lani and one of her brothers from their parents' home and placed them with a sister and brother-in-law.

"What's really strange," says Lani, "is that my dad's only been gone four years. It's not that long ago. But I feel like his death took a back burner because afterwards, we were dealing with my mother and then, later, her illness."

Lani says that she is still bereft from the loss of her mother this past year and that she is having a much harder time with her mother's death than she did with her father's. Yet, when she speaks about her father, Lani begins to cry. "He relied on me to be my mother's caretaker once he was gone. He trusted me. I always knew he loved me, despite his drinking. He wasn't really there much of the time because of his drinking but I never felt that he didn't love me. None of us ever felt that he didn't love us."

For Seth, Lani's older brother, their mother's death was the catalyst for completing unfinished business. "I think what made it harder for me when my mother died was that I hadn't finished grieving my father," says Seth, a veterinarian. "His death was more difficult because he was such a diminished person by the time he died. A lifetime of alcoholism and then he had finally dried out. But then he got sick. After he died, I thought I was doing okay. About a year later, a very close friend of mine, a kind of father figure to me, also died. I just kept moving ahead, not paying attention to all of the things I should have."

Seth goes on to talk about his mother at great length, how he was inspired by her strength and humor as she faced her death, though riddled with pain. He describes how she planned her funeral down to the last flower. But, like his sister, it is when he talks about his father that the tears finally begin to flow.

"I never had the opportunity to really enjoy my father and he never really got to be the father he wanted to be," Seth concludes, wiping the tears away. His wife, sitting nearby, reaches to take his hand. Seth, like his sister, is now actively grieving his father's death.

Sharing the Stories

"What helps people? Letting them talk about the deceased, that's what," says Jill of her experience as a midlife orphan. "I organized a study group on grief and loss at our church after my mother died. It was helpful although I think there's a limit on what people can understand until they experience it."

One very effective way that adult orphans deal with their loss is by sharing memories of their parents and their childhood with siblings, spouses, and friends. When I first began to seek adult orphans to interview, I felt like an anomaly. Most of my friends had at least one living parent. Sure, we often spoke of our families but the drive to reminisce was stronger for me. I found myself swapping stories about my family with my aunt, my mother's sister.

Since I also had lots of memories I didn't care to share with anyone, I assumed others would feel the same way. Perhaps that's why I was so overwhelmed by the avalanche of responses to my requests for adult orphans to interview. From all over the country, I received faxes, e-mail, and calls from people wanting to participate. More astonishing was the intensity of emotion I witnessed as people told their stories, some many years after the last parent's death.

Interviewees showed me family photographs and pointed out china and carpets that were inherited from parents. Typically, interviewees thanked me enthusiastically for the opportunity to reminisce. "It's something you don't get a chance to do very often. Most people aren't interested," says Phil. His wife, Elaine, also an adult orphan, nods her head in agreement.

In 1990, Paul Rosenblatt and Carol Elde conducted a study to probe the dynamics of shared reminiscence between siblings about a deceased parent. These researchers found that all of the respondents in their survey had engaged in shared reminiscence about a parent who had died. All but one felt that sharing memories was personally important. Yet, the researchers concluded, shared reminiscence did not seem to be a societal ritual, because in most cases, reminiscence was not formally recognized or planned for. While some families seem to have a ritual of shared reminiscence, for most people, it just happens.[14]

Talking about our parents helps us to work through our grief, to look at unresolved issues and learn more about the individuals who raised us. Many of the midlife orphans I spoke with were not particularly close to siblings, either geographically or emotionally. Some joined bereavement groups. Others talked to spouses or friends about their parents and their recollections. Everyone was eager to share with me.

When we share memories and stories, we start to come to terms with the individuals that our parents really were. Of the hundreds and hundreds of memories, most of us tend to select certain ones to recall. By sharing these stories, we may revise the way we perceive our parents and, sometimes, plug a new and often kinder ending onto the story of their lives. That is how Brian, a forty-nine-year-old accountant, was able to reshape his image of his parents.

Brian had long harbored anger at his father for allowing his mother to dominate the family with her emotional instability and alcoholism. "I think an element of grieving is going back and picking up the pieces and trying to figure out who your parents were. It was helpful to talk to the woman who worked for my father for so many years. I was surprised by how highly this woman regarded my father."

Pointing to the wall, Brian says, "That plate up there is signed by all of the people who were at my father's retirement party and he's got a whole book of what people wrote. I'm also going to talk to someone who was a neighbor of my mother's to get another perspective, to see how people saw my parents."

What Do We Grieve?

When our last parent dies, grief is not limited to the loss of the person. We grieve for many things—our youth, our other parent, our family of origin, and our own mortality. It's not unusual that, along with this mix, dependency issues and adolescent anger re-surface. Who takes the brunt of this attack? Of course, the last parent to die. "How could you leave me like this?" rages the surviving adult child. In this sense, the death of the second parent is uniquely different from other losses.

When her father died, Olga, in her mid-forties, found herself dealing with issues that she believed were buried long ago. Having grown up an only child in a home filled with dissension, Olga often walked a tightrope between her parents. Her parents divorced when she was thirty-two. After her mother died seven years later, Olga assumed her father would be around for a very long time. When he died just a few years after her mother, Olga's first reaction was hostile.

She relates, "I was always closer to my father because my relationship with my mother was so charged. Dad was my protector and nurturer. As he aged, his health started to fail but I really believed he'd be around for a while. When I got the call that he was sick, my initial reaction was anger. I was incredibly busy with my work and I thought, 'I can't just drop everything.' "

Olga is not a selfish, bad daughter. Her anger, as she later realized, was the resentment of the only child, dependent on parents who let her down so many times. As Olga explained, once she acknowledged the residual pain of her childhood, she was able to move on. Eventually, Olga established a memorial scholarship in her father's name.

Will had every reason to be furious with a father who essentially abandoned his wife and children. Yet, surprisingly, Will experienced anger not when his father died, but years later, upon his mother's death.

"I didn't go through a grief cycle when my father died," explains Will, a history professor. "I was separated from my second wife at the time and a lot was going on. I had two kids; one was from a previous marriage."

Will provides some background. His father was in the Navy and wasn't home much when Will was young. When he was around, he drank a lot and used to humiliate Will and his brother. When the boys were in elementary school, their father had an affair and subsequently left their mother. Later, their parents divorced.

"Divorce was unheard of in the fifties. I was very angry with my father. Much later, we reunited. I thought about him a lot when he died but I doubt if I really grieved.

"It was different when my mom died eight years later. I was really angry because I hadn't been able to communicate with her what I needed and then it was too late. I missed her greatly and was very sad, but my anger surprised me. I was angry over what I hadn't had, the nurturing I didn't really get from her."

It's interesting that Will describes a basically carefree, happy childhood in which his mother took care of her sons, despite the lack of financial security. As he continues to work through his grief, Will's anger toward his mother is tapering off. At some point, Will's perceptions may change and he will begin to accept a reality that is different from the one he now recalls. It may take even more time but Will is making headway.

Chris, whose last parent died two years ago, is doing the same. "I often pretend I'm talking to my parents, so I guess I miss them. Sometimes in my aloneness, I shout and scream into a pillow. That's what I do about my anger towards them."

Chris's very affluent but very alcoholic parents provided their children with material comfort and a fine education at prestigious prep schools and private colleges but they were totally unavailable emotionally. Now that their parents are gone, Chris and his six siblings struggle with various issues centered around their relationship with their folks. Many of the siblings have been married and divorced several times and some are in recovery from alcoholism or sexual abuse. One brother, an accountant, says he feels totally overworked as the trustee for their parents' complex estate and hurt by the others' seeming indifference to his efforts. A sister, in her early forties, is desperate to have a child and depressed by her inability to get pregnant. A brother is floundering professionally, searching for the career that will sustain his interest or enthusiasm. Another sister would like to have more of a relationship with her siblings but feels rebuffed by several of them.

All of the siblings are undergoing midlife changes and dealing with midlife issues, yet all relate some of the current angst to the death of their parents. They are grieving for their parents but their grief is centered on these midlife issues, assuming many forms—anger, resentment, depression, increased drive, and just plain old, ordinary sorrow for what never was.

In many cases, the loss of the last parent ends a very special relationship that has been a lifetime in coming, making this loss particularly difficult to endure. After the first parent dies, the adult child often develops a closer relationship with the surviving parent, sometimes getting to know the parent in a way that he or she hadn't before. Cass found that she and her father developed a warmer relationship after her mother, a good but emotionally withholding woman, died. For Jill, the time with her mother, her last parent, provided a healing period. Jill explains, "I put my life on hold to spend time with my mother at the end. We talked about the conflict we had had for so long and we were able to forgive each other. As horrible as her illness was, it was a gift because it gave us the time to forgive."

Rituals and Ceremonies

In August 1997, my friends Ron and Reva became adult orphans when their mother succumbed to the cancer that had plagued her for more than a year. Mimi was the quintessential *bubbeleh* (this term, a derivative of *bubba* (grandmother), translates as "sweetie pie"), so popular with her children's friends that she was always included in parties and social events. She was a surrogate mother and best friend to her daughter-in-law, a much-loved grandmother and aunt, and a role model for the power of positive thinking. Just a few months before she died, weakened from a year of chemotherapy that she was adamant about driving herself to, this indomitable woman took her sixteen-year-old grandson to his driver's exam. When they got there and realized they had forgotten critical insurance documents, she insisted on driving home and back (a half-hour ride each way) to get the documents so that Zack could take the test that day.

When Mimi died, only the immediate family attended the graveside funeral service, in accordance with her wishes. But so many people wanted to pay their respects to this wonderful woman that Ron organized a memorial service at home the day after the funeral. For nearly two hours (captured on video), more than one hundred friends, family members, and coworkers shared their memories of this beloved woman. They extolled a woman who saw only the good in everyone, who was a great sport, willing to try new experiences, passionately devoted to her family, and who made the world's best chicken soup. It was an extraordinary outpouring, marked with tears, laughter, and the love that was Mimi's legacy. As one woman said after the service, "If I can get a tiny fraction of this love when it's my turn, I'll die happy."

The memorial service was a tribute to Mimi but, more than that, it allowed her family to experience the love and support of so many friends, something that the small, private funeral denied them. As an adjunct to the funeral, the memorial service was a fitting farewell that enabled friends and family to grieve as a community.

Rituals serve an important purpose. They provide closure and help us come to terms with the reality and the finality of death. A funeral or memorial service marks the beginning of a formal grieving period so that eventually we will be able to remember our loved one without pain. The ritual provides us with support from others that lets us know that we are not alone.

Dr. Dana Cable, a psychologist who specializes in grief therapy, notes that the more rituals are used in the time following a death, the better the recovery through the grief process seems to be. Says Cable, "I get people who, in a sense, have taken the easy way out or didn't go through the elaborate rituals, and later, there's a lot of regret." In those cases, a therapist creates "therapeutic bereavement rituals" to create rituals that were not done at the time of death.

Cable, himself a Methodist, comments that Judaism, in particular, offers rituals that center in on the grief and focus it to a particular time and activity—something that most religions are missing. The seven-day Shiva, or mourning period that follows a death, is a time of daily prayer, surrounded by family and friends. For thirty days, mourners wear a black ribbon. Weekly, for the next year, they recite a mourner's prayer. The unveiling of the headstone, generally at the end of a year, marks the end of the formal grieving. However, each year the anniversary of a loved one's death is marked with a memorial candle. The deceased are also remembered at certain times of the year with memorial candles and prayers. While we don't need rituals to remember the dead, they help us to nurture the memories in the comfort and context of community. They remind us that we are not alone.

How we deal with the last parent's death is often quite different from the way that we handled the first parent's death. Minus a surviving parent, it is up to the adult orphan, either alone or with family members, to make decisions about the way the last parent will be memorialized and buried. When parents leave specific directions or have shared their wishes, this task is fairly straightforward. But it is not always so simple.

Planning a funeral can be a formidable responsibility, especially for an adult child who has never dealt directly with death. Some individuals are too overwhelmed to make these kinds of decisions. The pressure is tremendous because decisions must be made quickly. For others, planning the funeral or memorial rites for our last parent is a positive experience, albeit sorrowful, for it enables us to feel very adult and to repay our parents for all that they did for us.

Jill's parents were divorced when she was in high school. Not until her father died did Jill and her brother, Mark, know that he had arranged to be cremated, which upset them. Their stepmother held a memorial service at the retirement community where they lived, and Jill and Mark each spoke at the service. But Mark was very troubled that there was "no place to go" to remember their father. He talked to his mother about his feelings and she agreed to be buried, when the time came, in a cemetery near Mark and his family.

Jill, who was born Jewish, converted to Christianity when she married. With her last parent's death, she finds herself turning to her Jewish roots to honor her parents in their tradition, one that she finds comforting. Jill and Mark planned a Jewish funeral in New York City (where their mother lived), according to her very specific instructions. Later, they held a memorial service in the small town where they grew up and where she was buried. When Jill comes to New York from Milwaukee where she now lives, she visits her mother's grave, leaving a pebble on the headstone, a Jewish tradition. She lights a memorial candle for each parent. She and Mark feel good about the way they handled their last parent's burial. The rituals have been important to their sense of family and have helped them cope with their grief.

Margot was only seven when her father died. Although there was a funeral, his body was cremated and his ashes buried in his hometown in another state. Margot's mother never talked about her own burial wishes, even when she became sick. When their mother died, Margot and her sister assumed that she wanted to be cremated like her husband and her own mother. Each sister took some of the ashes to sprinkle in certain places that held emotional ties for them, but they buried the bulk of the ashes next to their father's during a small service with just family members in attendance.

A couple of months later, Margot organized a memorial service at the church where she sings in the choir. The service was a "celebration of life," as Margot puts it. "The Choral Arts Society sang, it was a very musical event, and then we had a reception at my mother's house. She was never a person that wanted to make anything big out of anything, so the less you did, the better," explains Margot. "But I don't think she would have been disappointed."

Margot remembers that when her father died, the many people who offered their support were a real comfort to her mother, who tended to keep her feelings to herself. The memorial service in the city in which she and her mother lived provided an opportunity for Margot to grieve with family and friends, and to find the same comfort that a support system had provided for her own mother so long ago.

Making the Ritual Work

"Grieving is for the people left behind," says Brian, an only child who was left to arrange each of his parent's funerals. Brian's anger at the Catholic church, which had ousted his mother when she was younger, led him to plan a funeral for his last parent that blended his ethical beliefs with his mother's religious leanings. Although his mother had been reinstated by the church years later, Brian was bitter about the emotional suffering his mother had endured and he felt very strongly that the service had to be right for him.

"The thing I ended up dealing with first and foremost when she died was the service and how I wanted to handle that." Brian dealt with his moral conflict by working with the Protestant chaplain at his mother's nursing home, a woman who was helpful and supportive to both him and his mother during her stay there. Together, they created a service that blended two religions and ideologies. Brian invited his mother's priest to say a few words and he complied. The service was one that was comfortable for Brian, one that he felt honored his mother but, at the same time, allowed him to take care of his own needs.

Often, stepping to the helm means that we are forced to make very critical decisions without the input of our parents. For many midlife adults, a decision that is counter to our parents' preferences can feel like a betrayal. Like my friends Ron and Reva or like Brian, we must strike a balance between our own comfort level and what we know our parents would have wanted. The fact that we don't always have much time to ponder these decisions places enormous pressure on us. It's important to remember that healthy parents wouldn't want us to agonize. We may be altering their wishes, but this affords us the opportunity to create a kinder and gentler memory with love and respect for ourselves as well as for our parents.

t h r e e

INHERITANCE

*T*hanksgiving vacation. The kids and I are stretched out on the living room carpet, lounging in front of the fireplace. The logs are crackling and we're roasting marshmallows—it's definitely one of those freeze-frame scenes. Dan, home from college, takes the brass tongs from their holder and begins to stoke the fire.

"Someday, I'd like these fireplace tools," he remarks.

"I wanted them," Andy pipes up. He pauses, "And the piano, you know, when the time comes."

"No way, the piano's mine," replies his brother, vehemently.

I listen to them spar, amused by this argument especially since I'm the only one who plays the piano, which was a gift from my grandparents when I turned eight. My sons always resisted piano lessons, of course. It wasn't until his senior year in high school that Dan first expressed an interest in playing. Now living in a fraternity house, he's teaching himself, learning about scales and chords from musician buddies. He tells me he's signing up for a basic music course next semester. We've taken to jamming together when he's home, with Dan improvising over my melody.

I suggest to Andy that it seems fair for Dan to get the piano, given his burgeoning interest.

"Okay, but I definitely get the cat," retorts Andy. He scans the room. "And that chair, 'cause it reminds me of Mom-mom and Pop-pop, and the lamp with the bird." He points first to the porcelain cat perched by the fireplace, then to the wing chair that had long graced my parents' living room, and finally to the lamp on the console table.

"Do you mind if I get the lamp?" he asks his brother in an afterthought.

Dan, who could care less about the lamp (I am certain of this), shrugs.

In the past few years, we've talked a lot about the things I have inherited from my parents and the memories they hold for me. That, coupled with the fact that I am writing this book, makes this exchange less peculiar than it might otherwise be for kids this age. Although I chuckle at the bantering between my sons, I am struck by their earnestness. I wonder briefly what will happen when that "someday" is here. How attached will they be to these things that have been a part of their home?

My sons' distinctly different personalities are apparent, even in this lighthearted exchange. Andy, emotional and articulate, is a passionate collector—his room is filled with *chotchkes* and souvenirs that reflect his insatiable curiosity. Dan, mellow and staid, is more discerning. His wants are generally utilitarian and his tastes more refined—a state-of-the-art computer, a chenille throw for his room in the frat house, or a pair of Birkenstocks.

So how will my sons one day address the task of dividing up my possessions? In a spirit of solidarity bolstered by family history and fond memories? Or will they instead bow to petty rivalry like two sisters I read about. It seems that once the sisters had divided up their parents' twenty-four place settings of Meissen china service, they couldn't agree on who should get the gravy boat. Unable to decide, they entrusted it to the estate lawyer, who would send the gravy boat out by messenger to whichever sister was giving a dinner party. She was required to sign a receipt and return the dish later.[15]

It was a sad commentary, one that makes me cringe. When the time comes, I certainly hope that my boys will value their relationship over any one possession. Had Dan and Andy been in a situation like those sisters, I hope that one would have agreed to keep the gravy boat and the other would have agreed to make the gravy.

A Rite of Passage

When our last parent dies, one of the most difficult tasks we face is the division of family property. On the surface, this job is nothing more than a practical matter—"you get this, I get that." In reality, though, the division of our parents' property is a rite of passage laden with potentially wrenching emotional and psychological issues. Watching our parents get sick and die depletes us emotionally. Planning the funeral is wrenching. But it is the experience of settling the estate that brings us face-to-face with our new status in the family album and it can take its toll as family dynamics shift. For many of us, the experience itself is bittersweet as we are suddenly handed what took our parents a lifetime to accumulate. Without parents to intervene, it falls on us to negotiate our way through this process with our siblings. How we handle this significant rite of passage can have an enduring effect on the next stage of our lives.

The burden is on parents to make the decisions about how to divide up their assets, but if they haven't done this, the situation is ripe for anger, bitter arguments, and hurt feelings. Sometimes, relationships between surviving children can be fractured forever by these squabbles over the division of personal property. As Marian Sandmaier points out in *Original Kin,* if the sibling bond is harmonious, it is apt to be handled with minimal turmoil. "But," she writes, "for those with serious unresolved resentments, settling of a parent's estate can be traumatically divisive."[16]

Not long ago, I read a newspaper article about the many baby boomers selling off their inherited family heirlooms. Apparently, with today's less formal lifestyle, many adults don't want to be weighed down by precious jewelry that requires safety deposit boxes and insurance premiums, or sterling silver pieces and fine china and crystal that need plenty of storage space. After all, not everyone is like the daughter who selected multiple pieces of her mother's fabulous gems, turning down an enormous emerald ring only because "green is not really my color."

The lure of the stock market has contributed to this phenomenon of selling off heirlooms, especially for baby boomers who enjoyed freewheeling spending in the eighties and are now scrambling to catch up on their savings goals.[17] We may be getting rid of the family goods but usually that happens only after we've engaged in negotiations to get the goods in the first place. Clearly, there's more than money invested in the process of splitting up our parents' personal property.

In the nearly thirty years that she has been practicing law, Joanna Reiver, an estate attorney in Wilmington, Delaware, has often found herself playing therapist when she guides families through the business of writing wills and estate planning. "I tell clients that whatever they do is their decision and that I want to help them accomplish their goals. But sometimes when you do that, there's a lot of psychological stuff that comes up in helping them. It's a skill you learn. I encourage people to make a memorandum and list everything, specifying who gets what. I tell them to date it, sign it, and keep it with their important papers. I'll hold a copy if they want me to. But the number of people who do that is very small."

Even the best planning cannot always eliminate family tiffs. Siblings who are able to split a million dollars' worth of securities without a hitch get into heated arguments over the aluminum pots and pans, working out old sibling resentments as the legal bills mount. In fact, Reiver agrees that the tangible goods—the jewelry, the china and silver, and even the pots and pans—generate the most friction. She elaborates, "It seems to happen a lot with grandfather clocks. Everybody wants the grandfather clock. Each person has the perfect spot for it so they fight over it."

Nearly everyone knows a story about siblings who never spoke to each other again after their parents' estate was settled. Unfortunately, I witnessed that in my own family. When my grandmother died, my father argued with his siblings over the estate and I gather that there was some legal wrangling. There must have been a mountain of anger and miscommunication between the siblings because my father never spoke to his brothers and sister again. At the time, I was away at college but I remember badgering my parents for some explanation for the schism that would make sense to me. I knew that the argument wasn't merely over money or possessions, because my father was neither greedy nor materialistic. What he was, though, was extremely principled with a strong belief in right and wrong. He set an example for us by actions that were always consistent with his words. There wasn't a hypocritical bone in my father's body. Something in the process of settling his parents' estate ruffled his moral and ethical feathers, fanning the rivalry between the siblings long fostered by their parents. The sad result of this split is that my children have never met the cousins I grew up with and a whole side of my family remains unknown to them.

What happened to my father and his siblings? Why were they willing to become estranged for life over an oil painting, a gold pin, or a grandfather clock? I may never have the answer but I wonder if my father or his brothers and sister believed that the estrangement was worth it. Dad was loved and respected by many people for his kindness and gentle good humor. When he died, we were warmed by several hundred cards and phone calls. But the absence of even a note from any of his siblings seemed more than a pitiful shame. It was a tragic omission.

Yours, Mine, and Mine

When sibling relationships are strong, there is likely to be very little change after the death of the last parent. If anything, sisters and brothers who have been close are drawn even closer in their mutual loss. Sometimes, when siblings have not been particularly close or are even estranged, the death of the last parent cements a relationship as the family pulls itself together. However, a wobbly relationship is just as apt to fall apart when there are no longer parents to pull the siblings together. The catalyst for the final blow to an ailing relationship is often the division of parents' personal property. When parents played favorites with the children, possessions take on a symbolic value. If the sibling perceived as the "favorite" gets more of the goods, then the other sibling interprets that as a sign of less parental love. The "loser" turns his or her rage on the sibling, who always did and even now "gets it all."

Such was the case with Karen, fifty-one, whose older brother, Sam, was born soon after their parents lost their first child to a tragic playground accident. The parents were still in deep mourning when Sam was born and, while they were responsible care-takers, they were basically emotionally unavailable. By the time Karen was born, their parents were further along in the grief process and were able to enjoy their newborn more. Sam always felt that Karen received preferential treatment and he still believes that he was shortchanged emotionally by their parents. Karen acknowledges that her experience with their parents was much more positive than her brother's relationship with them. However, she attributes this not as much to birth order as to her more compliant personality. She describes Sam as a willful, stubborn child.

When their father died just two years after their mother, Sam picked terrible fights with Karen as they divided up their parents' possessions. The arguments centered primarily on their parents' extensive folk art collection. Karen feels that the tension was exacerbated by the fact that their parents had specified two particularly valuable pieces to go to Karen, because they had always been her favorites. In Sam's mind, Karen was again being singled out for special treatment. Although Karen understood the dynamic, she felt helpless to change it. Sam needed an equal division of the art to prove that he was as loved by their parents as Karen was. Karen offered her brother some additional pieces to keep the peace but the damage was done. It is five years since their last parent died. Sam and Karen keep in touch but their relationship remains superficial and is emotionally unsatisfying for each of them.

Of Grandfather Clocks and Grand Pianos

Grandfather clocks notwithstanding, it was a grand piano that appeared to be at the crux of the argument between Ray and his brother. In reality, the problem stemmed from something else. As the older, more responsible son, Ray, a college professor, was named executor of their father's estate. The family home and all of its possessions were willed to Ray rather than his younger brother, a bright, talented, but troubled man with a history of four failed marriages and bouts of alcoholism and drug addiction that landed him in jail more than once. Chad was to receive a farm and the interest from certain investments that would provide him with lifelong income. Chad did not dispute the proposed structure of the inheritance, but he argued with Ray over one piece of property—the elegant family piano.

Chad, who played the guitar, was more musical than his brother and felt that he should get the piano even though it was willed to Ray. Ray disagreed. He thought that the piano would be a beautiful asset to his home and he felt that his younger, irresponsible brother would not treat it as the valuable piece of furniture that it was. He feared that Chad might even sell the piano, which had been in the family for decades. Only Chad's untimely death in an automobile accident resolved the problem, but Ray admits, with a twinge of guilt, that the piano would have become a major issue. He would not have given it up to his younger, irresponsible brother, whom he believed had been coddled by their parents for much too long.

Similarly, the family piano became the focus of the sibling rivalry in Donna's family. Her raven-colored eyes flashing, Donna recounts how her older sister insisted on getting the baby grand when their mother moved to smaller quarters years before her death. Sally was the only one of the five children who did not play the piano, neither did her children, and, besides, she already had a piano in her home. But Sally was the one whose home had to be perfect and not coincidentally, she was the sibling who had always felt unloved and resented the siblings whom she felt were favored.

When their mother died, this same sister claimed the silver tea service, which Donna had purchased in Mexico years ago for their mother, who had given her the money to buy it. Now Donna felt it should be hers. The other siblings agreed and were particularly upset since Sally had taken the piano several years before.

Donna's mother's will divided her estate equally between her five children except for a few things that she specifically directed to each child. The siblings, who for the most part acted with little acrimony over the large household filled with a lifetime's accumulation of furniture, dishes, and collectibles, wound up arguing angrily over the silver tea service. When another sister phoned Donna and encouraged her to go get the tea service before Sally took it, Donna did just that.

Recalls Donna, "I drove to New York and took the tea service from my parents' house, feeling like a thief. It was crazy. I just wanted a few things—the tea service, a painting Mom did, some dishes, and a vase that my mother always had in the center of her table. I used to set the table—that was my job when I was growing up—so my mom knew which dishes I liked and she left those to me."

"You know," she sighs, shaking her head, "I read somewhere that even if a mother could weigh her love equally on a scale, the kids would still feel that someone got more and someone got less."

Donna doesn't feel that her mother favored any of her children. But the experience of Donna and her siblings is re-created in millions of families each year. Even parents who showed no favoritism cannot always prevent the jealousy that exists between their children.

Making It Work

Sisters. Brothers. Brothers and sisters. The oldest and the baby. Married and unmarried. Professional and blue-collar. Driven and laid-back. Fat and thin. Handsome and homely. Siblings come in all kinds of combinations and with all kinds of histories. Many of us have positive experiences with our siblings, despite our differences. For others, the problems are perpetuated by the differences. When our parents die, we are forced to interact with siblings in an adult way. Not all of us are able to rise to the occasion. Although the arguments and fights of our youth may have abated, our ambivalent feelings have not. It is no wonder that a task like dividing up our parents' property is so unsettling.

I asked the adult orphans that I interviewed about their experiences with dividing up their parents' property. Most reported that they did not have many problems settling their parents' estate or dividing up property. Yet, upon further questioning, many recalled a specific argument over some item that caused a rift. Many said they later regretted the unpleasantness. Only a few felt that the experience had done permanent damage to a sibling relationship.

What exactly was it that helped those families get through the process without a permanent breakdown? Several factors seemed to be at work. When the parents had specifically targeted certain goods to each child, there was less quibbling among the children. The children who had given thought to how they planned to divide up their parents' possessions and agreed on a method had fewer arguments. But most significantly, siblings with a good relationship felt comfortable arguing—a disagreement was not a threat to the relationship. These siblings shared a mutual give-and-take attitude. They were able to make trade-offs and nobody viewed the experience as a win/lose situation.

That Mark and his siblings felt this way becomes evident as Mark shares a story. After his father died, Mark became the executor of his estate. Mark and his brother and sister agreed to divide their father's estate equally although each of the siblings was in a very different position financially. For Mark, a successful consultant with a physician wife and grown children, the inheritance would have little impact on his lifestyle. But for his brother, the money would help pay for his children's college costs. The inheritance would allow their sister, who was struggling financially in a low-paying job, to pay off debt, make some improvements in her home, and put away some savings. Neither Mark nor his brother minded that their mother's jewelry had been split between their sister and Mark's daughter or that the sister had received more from their mother's estate than her siblings. There was, however, a singular, unlikely item that warranted negotiation between the siblings—a framed flattened box of pizza mix.

Mark obviously relishes this tale. His eyes twinkle as he begins, "It's a funny story. We were living overseas and my wife and I were on our way back from the Philippines. My brother came to meet us and we all camped out. Every few days, we'd go to the market and buy a bunch of supplies. One day Larry and I bought this packaged stuff to make pizza and brought it back to camp, announcing, 'We've got pizza.' Well, how do you make pizza in camp? It was a favorite family story. So we kept the box and finally I framed it. My mother sort of adopted it for their house. She loved the story and, from time to time, she would threaten to actually make the pizza. It's like a family heirloom and it floats from family to family. My father brought it here when he moved. I think it's hanging up at my brother's house right now. When I go up there this summer, I'll probably end up with it. It was a unifying silliness and we all knew it was silly but so what? It was very symbolic, kind of a neat thing."

Parents and Good Intentions

Not all of the problems that arise in dividing up property stem from sibling rivalry. Sometimes, well-intentioned parents who want to help their children leave more to one child for good reason. But since any child may attach emotional worth to the gift, the child who receives less may read in that a message of low worth, even though he had a good relationship with his parents. Attorney Joanna Reiver describes a female client who came from a rather economically deprived background. Her husband, who was quite wealthy, gave her money to start her own business. She turned out to be a savvy businesswoman and became quite successful. When her parents saw that their daughter was financially secure, they eliminated her from their will, preferring to leave their assets to her sister, whose family was struggling.

It was true that the first daughter was financially comfortable; nonetheless, she was terribly hurt when she discovered that she had been cut from her parents' will. Regardless of her success, this woman wanted the emotional validation of her parents' love that she felt an inheritance provided. She wouldn't have cared if her parents had given her less than her sister, but being left out completely was quite painful.

Similarly, Danielle's mother planned to leave her estate to her other daughter, a widow, rather than to Danielle, a teacher married to a successful accountant. Danielle explains, "My parents always had this idea that you give to the weak, not to the strong. After my father died, my mother suggested that I sign over my share of the business that my father had left to me, my sister, and her son, because I had a husband to take care of me."

That decision didn't feel right to Danielle. Danielle spoke frankly to her dying mother and requested that she leave her something, saying, "Our circumstances can change. Les and I may not always be together. And what about your grandchildren? Don't you want to leave them something?"

Her mother listened respectfully to her daughter and honored Danielle's wishes. Eventually, Danielle and her husband bought out her sister and nephew's share of the business, establishing a trust that would guarantee a perpetual income for her sister. The remainder of the money helped pay for college expenses for Danielle's nephew. Danielle was fortunate that she was able to communicate her needs to her mother in time to prevent the painful result of being cut out of the will.

Parents with considerable assets often create a trust to protect the assets from taxes. But there are other reasons to establish a trust. Some experts argue that parents who set up trusts do not trust their children or have a great need to control them, even in death. While that is not always the case, circumstances sometimes dictate that a trust is a better way to protect the assets for adult children who have demonstrated poor judgment.

Marvin Roffman, a registered investment advisor and president of Roffman Miller Associates in Philadelphia, has seen his clients go to very creative lengths to protect their children from abusing or mishandling an inheritance. He tells of a client who left an estate in excess of seven million dollars. This man suspected that if he left a lump sum to his son, then thirty years old and somewhat shiftless, he would become even lazier and embark on a spending frenzy. The father set up a trust, stipulating that his son had to be gainfully employed and file an income tax return every year in order to receive any income from the trust.

The Executor Experience

At no point are sibling dynamics more evident than when the estate executor is named. The executor typically works with a lawyer or bank to locate and value the assets, pay the taxes, divide up the property, and carry out the directions in the will. The job usually lasts anywhere from one to three years but it may last much longer. The time frame does not necessarily reflect the size of the estate—it depends more upon how much the executor is willing to take on and how well the family communicates. As Ray explains, it's been six months since his father's death (which followed his mother's by just a few years) but as executor, he's still working on estate matters. He says, "I'm trying to deal with my parents' estate. During my father's last years, there were a lot of mistakes made and I'm trying to correct those. Thankfully, we didn't have to probate a will, which is a considerable amount of stress and strain. But I've been trying to get all the bills paid out. Over the last couple of years, I've had to go home about eleven times (hundreds of miles away) to take care of things."

Although the executor performs a business function, the appointment of one of the children as executor is frequently regarded as an act of favoritism. According to paralegal Faith Bracha, "All the personality clashes come through when parents name the executor, especially depending upon how it's handled. I think it's real important that the person who's chosen as executor can communicate. All the siblings should know who's been chosen. It shouldn't come as a surprise."

Joanna Reiver tells me about one of her clients who had six children and wouldn't choose one to be the executor because she feared it would cause animosity. Despite the fact that one of her daughters would clearly have been a great executress—she was extremely capable—the woman instructed her attorney to wait until she died to make the selection. "After she died," Reiver recalls, "the kids got together and they chose the one they all liked the most, who happened to be totally incompetent, completely disorganized—what a disaster. They spent so much more money that they should have because of poor communication."

Often the executor takes on the role of mediator, as Jay did after his father died. Adopting a tack similar to his parents' nononsense approach to child rearing, Jay simply laid out the rules to his siblings. "If I find anything or see anything that we're fighting over, I'm going to break it. I'll smash it in front of anybody because you have to remember what our parents would have wanted. If we fight over money, I'm donating every penny to charity. I won't tolerate it." Defending his stance, Jay explains, "None of us needed the money, it wasn't that much. We had heard so many horror stories about this process, so many negative stories of brothers and sisters not talking to each other. We had some time to think about it and talk about it beforehand. I think that's important to do."

A family in which the sibling relationship is strong generally does not succumb to rivalry or greed. Each member values the family cohesiveness more than the need for any tangible possession and each leaves his or her ego at the door. Siblings also maintain cordiality out of respect for their parents, particularly when parents have taken the time to discuss the matter with their children and to make their wishes clear. Lawyer, writer and entrepreneur Bryan Bell said his father cautioned that if his kids got into arguments over his estate, he'd kick the top off his coffin.[18]

You can bet those siblings didn't fight.

Eeny, Meeny, Miney, Moe

If siblings can limit the squabbling over their parents' possessions, the process of settling an estate is much less stressful and emotionally draining. With vital supportive relationships intact, brothers and sisters can continue to help each other through the grieving process and begin to heal together.

Jill recalls her experience with her brother when their last parent died. "When my grandmother died, my mother and her two brothers didn't speak to each other for a decade over splitting things. We didn't want that to happen. One thing helped—we didn't try to do it too soon. We delayed the process for a month or two. It had a lot to do with who we are and who we are with each other. We made our minds up not to fight about this. And we didn't. We sat down and my brother said, 'What would you like?' Both of us gave in on some things."

One of the most helpful things a family can do to reduce the tension is to decide ahead of time how they are going to divide the personal effects. The method we use isn't as important as the fact that everyone is in agreement. Some families get an appraisal of valuable jewelry, antiques, and furniture and prefer to treat the property division in terms of cash value, with each sibling getting an equal amount. Phil's parents, who had accumulated many pieces of jewelry and furniture of significant value, included an insurance appraisal in their wills so that Phil and his siblings knew the value of each piece prior to dividing up their parents' things.

Most of the adult children I interviewed had opted to split up the personal property by sentiment rather than by cash value. Each family adopts its own procedure for the process—some are rather creative. A relatively standard method is for family members to draw straws to decide who goes first and then alternate choosing pieces. A clever twist on this method allowed members of one family to draw straws and let each person make one selection. Then the order reversed, with the last to choose going first in the next round. After each go-around, the order reversed until everything had been selected.

Another family of two heirs tossed a coin. The winner was

given the choice of either making the first selection or going second with the option of selecting two items. After the first pick, the siblings proceeded to alternate.

One family handed out tags, a different color to each sibling. They simply went around and marked what they wanted with their tags. This works until siblings want the same thing. What happens then? Kiki ran up against this very issue with her sister.

Kiki recalls the day she and her sisters began to divide up their parents' things. "Mom was an artist. She had about forty paintings. We laid everything out all over the apartment and then pulled numbers out of a hat. We just went in numerical order. My mom had promised me a certain painting but my sister wanted it also. We turned it over and Mom had written my name on the back so that settled it."

Kiki and her sister were fortunate that their mother had had the foresight to make her wishes clear, thus eliminating an argument. When that doesn't happen, it is up to the siblings to negotiate or to spend the assets on an attorney.

Most estate lawyers agree that it is not a good idea to let in-laws or spouses sit in on property divisions. If siblings want spouses involved, then all must agree.

When There Are No Siblings

Generally, only children do not have to worry about sharing an inheritance. But that doesn't mean an inheritance has less emotional impact for them. For many only children, the death of the last parent magnifies the degree of aloneness. There may be more possessions than one person wants or can use, yet there is no sibling to share them with. It may be difficult to give away possessions that were important to our parents or a part of the home for so many years. While the emotional tie is there, the item may not be something that suits our taste or fits into our décor or lifestyle, yet giving it away invokes guilt.

Sometimes, the child who is left with all of her parents' possessions will look for ways to divest herself of some things of sentimental value without feeling guilty. Bess did that after her mother's death two years ago when she was left with her mother's home and all of its contents. She explains, " I found my mother's high school yearbooks. She was the valedictorian of the class of 1927. At the time, there were very few blacks in the school. I gave one to the museum [of black history] and one to the school in case they don't have one in their archives. I also found an award she got—it's a glass cylinder, like an oil lamp, that says, 'Keep your light shining.' I'm going to box it up and send that to my niece in Germany because I thought she might like to have it. I get lots of satisfaction and comfort from doing those kinds of things for my mother. I gave some plates to a woman she worked with who had been very nice to her.

"My parents had a house full of furniture that they loved but most of it went to auction. I kept a few things but I didn't want to turn my house into my parents' house. While I have things in my house that were theirs, this is mine."

Miriam, also an only child, felt that it was important to bury her mother with some of her personal items but she was torn between burying certain things and keeping them, afraid that she might regret losing them. In the end, she selected some personal letters, a few of her mother's porcelain dolls, and a bracelet that her children had given their grandmother to place inside the casket. Miriam also wanted her children to have a remembrance of their grandparents, so when her mother died, she gave her parents' rock collection to her young son. Miriam's daughter keeps her grandmother's collection of porcelain dolls on display in her room.

While an inheritance can significantly improve one's circumstances, it may also evoke uncomfortable feelings, especially for the only child who feels so alone, as Miriam did. Miriam, whose parents had encouraged her dependency, was overwhelmed at having to sell her parents' home by herself. But in doing so successfully, she discovered that she could be quite capable. Without siblings to share with, Miriam inherited enough money from the sale that she and her husband were able to buy a bigger house. Miriam invested the remainder of the money and receives regular income. However, Miriam, whose last parent died less than a year ago, says she hasn't really enjoyed the new house because she's so sad that her mother can't see it. Struggling with her ambivalent feelings, Miriam recounts a recent dream in which someone calls to say her mother had not died after all and then her mother calls to complain that "you sold my house." She acknowledges that she is relieved to have an inheritance, because her husband does not earn much, but she is uncomfortable that this gain is the result of her parents' death. What's particularly interesting is that Miriam is not willing to share the remainder of her inheritance with her husband, who holds down two jobs. Her unwillingness has added to the already present friction between the couple.

Randi is the product of very fiscally prudent, conservative parents of the Old South. Although the family was quite comfortable, they did not believe in indulging their only child, who was given a modest monthly allowance from the time she started high school. From this source, she was responsible for her lunch money, bus money to school, her own clothes, and any incidental expenses. When her parents died, Randi was left with a substantial inheritance. Randi, like Miriam, has chosen not to share her inheritance with her husband, maintaining that it is her money.

That both of these women—only children—have decided not to share their inheritance with their spouses may be purely coincidental. On the other hand, it may be an issue that warrants further exploration.

Parents Who Have Remarried

What happens when parents have remarried? How do these families handle inheritance? The lawyers who serve them stress the importance of full disclosure. Imagine what it's like for an estate attorney, interviewing a surviving spouse, to learn for the first time that the deceased has a child from a previous marriage. Navigating through the waters of second marriages can make siblings who are settling their parents' estate wish for a good life preserver.

Some families, like Jay's, are lucky. Jay and his siblings had an excellent relationship with their stepmother. She respected their memories and their ties to their nuclear family. When Mary married their father, she suggested that he give his children many of the belongings he had shared with his first wife—china, silver, crystal, and collectibles. Mary, a widow, brought to the union her own things, collected over the lifetime of her first marriage. She reminded her stepchildren that "I didn't marry your dad for your mother's possessions." When their father died, Mary called to offer his antique watch to Jay and to ask if there was anything else he or his siblings wanted.

Not all children are so fortunate. Remarriage (whether it is the parents or the children who have remarried) opens up the proverbial can of worms. The question of what is fair prevails in many aspects of second marriages but is especially predominant in the area of inheritance. Adult children, like Heidi, struggle to find adequate solutions to these problems. Heidi, whose father died when she was in college, is divorced and remarried with two stepdaughters. Her father's estate was in a trust with a lawyer as the executor. The family agreed that her brother would be the executor for their mother's estate and, eventually, they also agreed on dismantling the father's trust. Heidi explains, "My mother didn't want our inheritance to go to my stepdaughters. She wanted it to go to my brother and me. My husband and I had an argument over it—he couldn't believe I wouldn't share it with his girls. I ended up spending much of my inheritance right away just so I didn't have to deal with setting up another trust."

A friend of mine, a very reasonable and unselfish woman, shared with me a current issue in her family. Her parents divorced nearly twenty-five years ago. A year later, her father married a woman with three children from her previous marriage. Now retired and with all of the children grown, my friend's father and stepmother are writing new wills. Because they have always merged their money, they are questioning how to share their assets equitably. The father's income was considerably higher than his wife's. Should they divide their assets evenly between the five children or should they divide the assets in half, leaving one half to his two daughters and the other half to her three children? I asked my friend what she felt would be fair. She responded, "It's not enough money to really make a difference in my life. But I do feel that my sister and I should get half. Whatever they decide, it won't change my relationship with my stepbrother and stepsisters—we get along well. But I feel like we should get half of my dad's assets. That seems fair to me."

Who's to say what is fair in this case? How will the mother's three children feel about a fifty/fifty split with their two stepsiblings? It is possible that some of the children will be unhappy with their decision, no matter what it is. But by confronting the issue and discussing it with the children, these parents have taken a big step toward eliminating ill will between the stepsiblings.

A task that is normally charged with emotion becomes even more loaded when there is a surviving stepparent with whom there has never been a good relationship. For Chris and his siblings, their grieving for their parents has been exacerbated by estate problems with the woman he refers to as the "stepmonster." Chris's father married Chloe, a family acquaintance, just months after his wife died. Although all of the children had a troubled relationship with their mother, an emotionally distant woman, they were distraught over their father's remarriage to a woman they neither liked nor trusted. The siblings agree in their assessment of their father as a weak individual, easily led and manipulated. They feel that his second wife turned him against his children.

Soon after the marriage, at his new wife's urging, their father sold the home on the jagged New England coast where generations of the family had gathered for summer vacations. This decision produced great consternation for the children. He also distanced himself from the sons with whom he had always shared his financial dealings. When he died, Chloe retained most of his things of value. His children are left sorting out their feelings of resentment toward their father and Chloe as well as emotions they have kept under lid since dividing up their mother's possessions several years earlier.

Secondary Fallout

Herb, the oldest of the siblings and executor of their father's estate, watches as the tension between his siblings develops. He has seen them separate into camps—some very businesslike, some more humanitarian. He recalls the time after their mother died. "My mother didn't leave specific possessions to anyone. Whatever tangibles my father didn't take, we [the siblings] shared. My brothers who live on the West Coast didn't get anything because they weren't present. I got a coffee table and a TV. One of my sisters said we should put our names on anything we want but then she pulled up in a U-Haul and filled it. I can tell you after the fact that there's resentment from those who got less."

Ronni, a sister, remembers it somewhat differently. "My sisters, my oldest nephew, and one brother and myself were involved in splitting up some of the stuff. It ended up that there was a lot of anger over how that was done. My brothers were angry with us. We asked them what they wanted and said we'd send it to them but they never said anything. It was different when my father died. He had named certain things to go to certain people, so the last time we all got together to divide up some of his things, we tried to do it better. My stepmother's still in possession of lots of things, however."

When she reflects on the family heirlooms, of which there were so many that at times her parents stored them in a warehouse, Ronni comments that perhaps her parents didn't believe that their sons and daughters had attachments to anything in particular. They never asked their children what they would like to inherit. Several times throughout their lives, this affluent couple donated pieces of their fine furniture to charitable organizations. In fact, Ronni admires this aspect of her mother. "She gave away some priceless antiques to this community center where she used to work. She didn't think about her kids or about passing things down through the generations. I love that legacy—she was kind of this Robin Hood character."

Their mother did not bequeath everything to those less fortunate. About ten years prior to her death, she parceled out many of her valuable jewels to her daughters. After her death, the girls shared the remainder of the jewelry, assuming that their brothers weren't interested. Ronni admits, "I have felt some guilt about that. So far, there hasn't been any flak although we've had some discussions about whether it was fair." She continues, "Also, one of my sibs had borrowed a lot of money from our parents over the years and we've all had fights about that. My parents never kept things equal so now we're trying to sort out who owes what to whom. We've all inherited money. In a way, our parents bought our love. Some of us asked them for money and got it. Others got a boot in the face. Once I asked for a loan and had to pay it back right away but the two who got the big loans were the favorites."

It is evident that the siblings in this family are not going to have an easy time dividing up their parents' assets and property. With eighteen years between the youngest and the oldest and a family history of sexual abuse and alcoholism, there is no doubt that these siblings have some serious issues with each other and their deceased folks.

The middle child, Chris, is apparently the family peacemaker and the one "who wants everyone to love him," according to one of his siblings. Chris clarifies that the gifts he and his siblings received during their parents' lives assured them opportunities that most people don't have. They didn't need to drive old clunkers. They were able to buy homes at a young age. They could make career choices that were not dependent upon salary. Still, Chris describes his inheritance with some disdain.

He explains, "Our parents were very wealthy and when I was growing up they had several homes. By the time they died, there wasn't much left. My father chose to give a lot of their money to his alma mater, which he had attended on a full scholarship. He didn't think that the kids needed all of that money. My parents lived very well. Their priority was to take care of themselves. My father never discussed the living trust he set up for his second wife with us. For the first four years after Mother died, my brother and I were in charge of his assets, making sure they were properly invested. I was in the financial business at the time. But in the last year of his life, my father turned away from us."

Not only is Chris angry at his parents, he has some negative feelings about his sisters. "My father sold the beach house and told my sisters to go take what they wanted. I asked for something specific but never got it. While it didn't cause that much trouble, it was more of a wake-up call about greed. I expected better. My sisters said they didn't realize that people wanted things and that we (the brothers) just had to let them know. I ended up getting a bureau but we're talking about a full house of furniture—the bureau was a token of appeasement. My sisters also took all of my mother's jewelry. She had superb brooches, bracelets, necklaces, and rings. I have no idea of the value of her jewelry but it's all gone."

I listen to these sisters and brothers and I hear them struggling to make sense of their anger and pain. Each is financially secure, despite however shortchanged he or she may feel about the inheritance. Underscoring the anger and resentment is the longing for what Chris and his siblings really want from their parents and will never have—the legacy of a home filled with caring, concern, and love.

Dollars and Sense

Each year, nearly one billion dollars' worth of property passes through America's probate courts. Most of it is conveyed through trusts and estate plans, making estate planning a $600 billion industry. Thanks to a generation of thrifty parents who believed in saving more than spending, the next twenty years will see an unprecedented ten trillion dollars passed between generations.[19] The transfer of money and property creates a range of choices and opportunities for the surviving adult child. Adult orphans agree that one benefit of their changed status is the newfound security of an inheritance.

For middle-class adults like John, an inheritance can lighten the burden of family expenses. Although John's mother was left with little money when her husband was murdered in a holdup, she managed to hold on to her house, her most important asset. When she died twenty years after her husband, John used his portion of the proceeds from the sale of her house to pay for the funeral and to put his son through college.

In her mother's will, Maura received an option to buy her parents' duplex at the beach. Maura and her husband got three separate real estate appraisals for her sisters and when they all agreed upon a price, Maura and her husband exercised their option. By renting out the property, they have produced additional income. They will be able to buy the house they want sooner than they had planned.

For Margery, a forty-nine-year-old single woman, her parents' estate supplied her with a nest egg that alleviated her fear and anxiety about growing old alone. With the cushion of her inheritance, Margery, a struggling photographer with a modest income, finally felt secure enough to rent the studio space she had long wanted. She gave up her part-time job so she had more time to market her work and to concentrate on doing what she did best— photography. Business increased substantially and, within a few years, Margery began to procure lucrative commercial projects.

An inheritance may provoke guilt feelings in us initially, particularly if our relationship with our parents was less than satisfactory or we were inattentive to them in their later years. Some adults are surprised to learn that their inheritance is quite substantial. An inheritance may reveal a side of our parents we had never seen. Some children become angry when they realize that their parents did not have to live as frugally as they did. As Cass, whose inheritance of nearly a half million dollars left her reeling, said, "My father used to take my ailing mother to the doctor across town on two buses rather than hire a taxi. I always thought he did things like that because their financial resources were limited. Now I find out it's because he was too cheap. I don't know what they were saving all that money for. So they could leave it to me?"

Cass, who enjoyed a warm relationship with her parents, concedes that their "cheapness" probably stemmed from a Depression mentality. Nevertheless, she has some residual angry feelings about the way they lived so meagerly. It is not that she isn't grateful for her inheritance, Cass explains, but, "I would have preferred that my parents had lived better, spent more of the money on themselves and had some fun with it."

What to Do with Your Inheritance

Not everyone is thrilled to suddenly own an original oil painting or to become the lord of a one hundred-thirty-acre farm that's been fallow for three decades. Perhaps you don't want to be bothered unloading a ramshackle mountainside fixer-upper thirteen hundred miles away or you detest the garish modern paintings that your parents loved. If you are one of those rare birds who choose to disclaim their inheritance for any reason, notify the executor as soon as possible. Don't wait—there are time restrictions and you may be forced to accept your inheritance. Most of us, however, will be more than glad to see an inheritance as the gift it is meant to be. Depending upon the form of the bequest, an inheritance can catch us off guard. Often, heirs who need money resent an inheritance that is tied up in a physical asset, not particularly liquid, like an original sculpture or an eighteenth-century chair. As we have seen, it is often the desire for cash that prompts children to sell off the family heirlooms. What then? What do you do with the money? And what do you do if you inherit a sum of money? How do you deal with the sudden windfall?

Experts advise that it is best to wait a while to make financial decisions. Put the cash into some kind of savings account with a reasonable interest rate or something accessible, like money market funds or short-term certificates of deposit. Whatever you do, take time to evaluate your options. Some heirs may decide to use their inheritance to benefit others. Some may elect to donate money to charities. If you wish to secure the future of your children or grandchildren, then you will want to establish a trust. A trust can be a complex planning tool and requires the help of experts like a tax attorney and an investment specialist.

Financial advisor Marvin Roffman says he never ceases to be amazed by the different attitudes that children within the same family have toward money. "I'm a trustee of an estate that provides for three adult children equally. One saves every penny and another takes all the dividends out and occasionally invades the principal. The other is a physician who has taken out money only because her husband is quite ill and requires unorthodox medical treatment that isn't covered by insurance."

Roffman, like other financial advisors, sits with his clients to determine their financial goals. They discuss obligations and make a wish list, taking into account the tax liability of the estate. Generally, an inheritance isn't dropped in our laps all at once. Assets must be probated (assessed by the state for taxation purposes). Stocks, bonds, and certificates of deposit must be transferred. Sometimes property must be sold.

Most investment advisors suggest that you develop a strategy for investing your money with the maximum return that is compatible with your risk tolerance. Decide what you want your money to do so you can choose appropriate investments.

Whatever you decide to do, bear in mind that if you use it wisely, an inheritance gives you the opportunity to make a significant difference in your life. Spending an inheritance on others may be tremendously fulfilling. On the other hand, careful planning can secure our old age. Actually, these two are not mutually exclusive. You may opt to do both.

As Roffman says, "Whatever you do, consider the future. Many people inherit enough to make life more comfortable with wise planning. Your parents were able to do that for you, weren't they? But don't deny yourself, either. I always tell my clients that this isn't a rehearsal. I've known people who died young. You don't have to deny yourself. After all, they don't put roof racks on coffins."

PARENTS AND CHILDREN

"He ceas'd, but left so pleasing on the ear, his voice that
listening still they seemed to hear."

—HOMER

$\mathcal{I}$t was a brilliant sunny day in
late spring of 1974. The usual cloying humidity had not yet ar-
rived in the nation's capital. My friend Howard and I were enjoying the perfect weather during one of our frequent lunchtime
strolls. I was in my late twenties, single, and a writer for a ven-
erable publishing concern. Howard was ten years older, married,
and a senior editor who had become my friend and confidant. As
we ambled up Massachusetts Avenue, we chatted about growing
up. The conversation took a sharp turn when Howard revealed
that both of his parents were dead. Uncomfortably caught off
guard, I murmured some sympathetic words.

Howard's response was not at all what I expected. Instead of
telling me how tough it was to have no parents, Howard remarked that it wasn't so bad; in some ways it made his life easier.
He was able to make his own decisions, based solely on what he
wanted to do and what felt right for him. His parents would never

have approved of his choice of spouse, he explained, but in fact his marriage made him very happy. I found his remarks disturbing, and for days I pondered them.

Nearly twenty-five years later, I often think back to that conversation. Each time I make a decision that spurns the parental voices in my head, I recall Howard's words and, finally, I understand. As reluctant as I am to admit it, there's a certain sense of freedom that springs from the autonomy of my orphan status. Margot, a professional photographer and adult orphan, describes this feeling: "For me, it's about being in charge of my own life, being totally responsible. It's coming up with an idea and not having to look over my shoulder to see if it's okay to do it."

How disconcerting to discover that the absence of parents not only generates a fierce longing for them but also frees us of feelings we may not even have known we had. As adult children, we can readily acknowledge strong ties to our parents but we don't generally consider ourselves dependent on them, especially as we assume an increasingly active role in their care. Yet, long after our parents are gone, their voices still whisper to us. Even without their physical presence, the relationship continues.

There is no telling when I first became aware of this newfound sense of autonomy, but I suspect it had its origin in the same arena as the feeling of abandonment I realized the night my last parent died. Not for a moment then could I have believed that I would ever see anything positive in my orphanhood. Nor does this new feeling mitigate the pangs of loss that I still experience. Yet it is undeniably there, a sense of self that is more confident, more independent, more "adult" now that I am without parents. How could I have anticipated feeling this way? Until my last parent died, I wasn't aware that I wasn't yet fully adult. Not that I'm much different from how I was before my parents' deaths, at least not noticeably. Long before my parents died, I made life decisions—career moves, marriage and divorce, child rearing choices—that I carried out my way. But throughout every step, the voices of my parents were present. I listened but ultimately I did what I felt was right for me. Sometimes we agreed, more often we didn't. How much easier it would have been had my parents supported all of my choices, but they had their ideas and opinions just as I had mine.

Now there's no longer anyone waiting in the wings to disagree or disapprove; conversely, there's no mother or father to turn to for support or to applaud for me. The resulting and somewhat surprising paradox is that while the loss of my parents still saddens me, it no longer disturbs me. Instead, orphanhood has become a kind of exhilarating challenge for me, as it has for so many other midlife adults.

How do we transform from the anguished orphan to the accepting, independent adult, no longer anyone's child? To say the process begins the moment we are born is hardly an overstatement. To understand it, we look back to our family of origin, for it is there that the metamorphosis finds its genesis.

Pondering the Original Connection

"Remember how good it felt to have someone take care of you when you were little? Feel it all over again," reads a newspaper advertisement for a managed care health plan. No dummies, those ad people. What an appeal—after all, who doesn't long for the warm, cuddly, cookies-and-milk comfort of childhood? Oh, the inexplicable longing for that earlier, secure time of our lives that floods us when our last parent dies.

Psychologist Emma Mellon of Rosemont, Pennsylvania, addresses the loss that provokes the sense of orphanhood, even among healthy adult children, this way: "I think it reminds us of the original connection with our parents from the time we were infants. The loss breaks through the defenses so that those old feelings of dependency and deep love rise up again. It doesn't matter what the relationship in the real world was, it's the picture of the relationship that the 'infant' has in its mind. In the beginning, it was overwhelmingly wonderful without any reasoning to temper that wonder, unless the child had been hurt at a very early age. I think loss just regresses us to the point where the things that are unconscious start getting conscious."

This explains why Lynda, a fifty-three-year-old administrative assistant who rarely shed a tear for most of her life, now cries "at the drop of a hat" since the death of her mother, her last parent. Lynda explains that her childhood was dominated by a mother whose behavior was completely unpredictable, sometimes very loving, and, just as frequently, withholding. Lynda regularly smothered her anger at her mother's inexplicable refusal to speak to her for days at a time and her father's passivity in not dealing with his wife's bizarre behavior.

During the last three years of her life, Lynda's mother stopped communicating with her. Although Lynda tried to make contact with her mother, her efforts were rebuffed. Several years ago, her mother died, alone in her apartment, where Lynda's brother found her body. Her death left Lynda both angry and relieved. Yet, when Lynda looks back, she prefers to focus on the good times when the family worked together at the restaurant they owned. She recalls fondly her mother's wonderful baking and skill in the kitchen. She finds herself poring through her mother's vast collection of cookbooks and enjoying baking much as her mother did.

Lynda says that she has never been one to cry easily or display much emotion. Since her mother's death, though, she frequently finds herself teary-eyed. She thinks often about her parents and her childhood, trying to make some sense of it and to figure out what to do with her ambivalent feelings toward her parents.

As part of her mourning, Lynda is reviewing her family history, mulling it over, sorting out the good from the bad. In fact, she is processing her thoughts in much the way that a therapist would help a client. Clinicians who work with grieving adult children direct the therapy to several of the tasks of mourning for this particular age group. These include (1) stocktaking, in which the adult child explores the initial changes caused by the death, (2) recalling both unpleasant and meaningful memories, and (3) internalizing these memories so the child can move on.[20]

It may not be easy at first, because we feel guilty, but expressing our ambivalent feelings about our deceased parents affords us a measure of comfort, and, at the same time, encourages our personal growth. Once we can talk about the present without denying the past, we can be certain that we have really known our parents. Really knowing our parents—that's what enables us to think of them gently. Once we can express the values that our parents have conveyed during our midlife, we are a lot closer to resolving their deaths. Whether or not we share their religious, moral and ethical convictions, their ambitions and their notion of family, we take a leap in our growth when we distinguish between that which was distinctly theirs and what is uniquely ours. Yes, we have done this work at other times in our development, but as midlife orphans, we do it willingly and with mature consideration.

The Developing Child

Of the many developmental theories about children that look at the interaction between children and their primary caregivers, especially during the first few years of life, one that is widely accepted is the object relations theory. This model of infant development emphasizes the impact of the child's early interactions with "objects" (people and things) on his later functioning and well-being.

According to the object relations model for the early phases of child development that was created by Margaret Mahler and colleagues, during the infant's first one to two months (the *autistic phase*), the little cutie in the crib is oblivious to everything except himself. In the next four or five months, he begins to recognize others but merely as extensions of himself, not as separate beings (the *symbiotic phase*).[21] When the baby cries and this woman appears on demand, he does not perceive her as "Mommy." As far as the baby's concerned, she is a part of him, an appendage like an arm or a leg.

This early period is followed by a *separation-individuation period,* extending through ages two to three years, during which the child starts to realize that "Mommy isn't me and I'm not her." It's during this phase that we establish a separate sense of self, drawing boundaries between self and others. Complicating this task is the ever-present conflict—"I need you near me" versus "Go away." Add the fear of being abandoned and the opposing fear of being engulfed and the result is one emotionally charged developmental task. As if this weren't difficult enough, further fueling the struggle to separate is the fact that the child sees the caregiver (generally the mother) as two separate beings: when she is comforting and sensitive, she is seen by the child as "all good"; when she is unavailable, she is perceived as "all bad"—not a particularly enviable spot for Mom.

Child development experts consider a child's ability to navigate through this phase to be crucial for later mental health. As the child develops, this splitting is replaced by a healthier integration of Mom's good and bad traits. Replacing separation anxiety is the knowledge that Mother or the primary caregiver exists even when she is not physically present—the phenomenon commonly known as *object constancy*. Thus, the toddler learns to tolerate ambivalence and frustration. He begins to appreciate the concept of unconditional love and acceptance. He becomes more responsive to Father and others in his world. His self-image becomes more positive. This is when we see a child lugging around an object like a blanket, a stuffed animal, or a doll—the object represents the constant figure and helps ease separations.

When Sammy finally gives up his "blankey," we can sigh with relief that he's been able to internalize a permanent image of a secure mother figure. It's a big step for Sammy. As Judith Viorst writes, "as long as we, not our mother, initiate parting, and as long as our mother remains reliably there, it seems possible to risk, and even to revel in, standing alone."[22]

For years, life rolls on with the somewhat predictable rhythm of childhood. And then comes adolescence. Once again, separation-individuation issues rear up as questions of identity and closeness to others again become concerns. In normal development, the adolescent will experiment and consciously test behaviors that are different or even oppose those of her parents. She searches for an identity that is uniquely hers. At the same time, she reacts to significant people other than Mom and Dad—teachers, peers, employers, or even the parent of a friend. This is the age when we struggle to separate from our parents more than just physically. We separate morally, intellectually, and psychologically. Wise parents know to tread carefully through these years. In the healthy family, parents help their offspring each step of the way to develop a positive self-image that ultimately enables them to reach out to others with love.

Not everyone is fortunate enough to come from a healthy family. Some of us had parents whose obsessive clinging or need to control hindered our growth. Often, what passes for the desire to keep the family close is actually a disguised fear of letting go or allowing the children to separate. And so we find adult children who grumble but who dutifully attend regular weekly dinners to appease parents who don't hesitate to make their displeasure known when opposed. Other parents push their children away in the pretense of making them independent. Often, these are parents who are uncomfortable with intimacy, perpetually "stressed out" or "too busy" or who are besieged by their own emotional problems.

When Jill, whose parents divorced when she was in high school, looks back at her childhood, she now sees how it was shaped by the conflict in her parents' relationship. "My mother said she wanted her kids to be very independent. My brother and I were very competitive and there was a lot of sibling rivalry. He was older and I wanted to do whatever he did. So at age seven, I went to sleep-over camp for eight weeks, like my brother. I can't imagine sending my eight-year-old son away like that."

Was Jill's mother encouraging independence or was it an excuse to relinquish her parental role as she struggled with her relationship with her husband? In his thoughtful book *The Soul's Code: In Search of Character and Calling,* psychologist James Hillman discusses the life of the family that doesn't engage in the kind of probing conversations that share values and judgments, regret and despair, as well as ideas and fantasy. These are the families in which so-called good parents subscribe to the notion of unconditional positive reinforcement and see that the child has his own room complete with TV and phone line. Of this behavior, Hillman writes, "the fantasy that governs these parental stupidities is distancing, euphemistically called independence."[23]

Ronni grew up in one such empty family. Her emotionally unavailable, wealthy, socialite parents provided a beautiful home, exclusive prep school education, and all the material finery for their children. "But," says Ronni, "by the time I came along, my parents were pretty deeply into their drinking, particularly my mom. As my mother became more incapacitated and out of control, it had a huge impact on their parenting. They were not very present as parents when I was growing up. But we had nannies—one woman in particular—that my family hired to take care of us all the time. So we sort of had substitute parents but there was always a sense of something missing. There wasn't that connection with my parents."

Ronni's parents didn't set out to ignore or dismiss their children. None of this behavior is intentional. Most parents want to be good parents. Ronni's sister Joan, a social worker, understands this. "I miss the thing I've always missed, which is the potential that they had to love us, or to love me. My reality is that it was never actualized. I think all parents mean to love their kids. I work a lot with parents to try to teach them how to do that. I think my parents meant to love me but they just didn't know how."

Good parenting doesn't come naturally, although, generally, the parenting we practice mirrors the parenting we had. That is not to say that the parenting we experienced seals our future as a parent, or our future in general. Other factors, of course, intervene—an individual child's personality, relationships with siblings, birth order, trauma such as illness, death, or moving, changes in environment, and myriad other circumstances. And, fortunately, parenting is a skill that we can learn and perfect. Many adults who come from dysfunctional homes have learned to be effective parents. Whatever kind of parenting we did have, it is probable that our parents were doing the best they could.

The bottom line is that we all grow up, in spite of our childhood experience. And humans are remarkably resilient. But that primary relationship with our parents will continue to influence us in one way or another for the rest of our lives. By the time we reach adulthood, the success or lack of success of the early developmental period still resonates. We become competent artists, plumbers, musicians, office workers, teachers, lawyers, computer analysts, and even leaders of large companies. To the world, it appears that we are grown-up, independent adults, but behind closed doors, our struggles with addictions, troubled relationships, or gnawing self-doubt reveal a different profile. For many adults, there is still work to do, as evidenced by the millions of adults who seek therapy each year. Psychologist Emma Mellon explains, "When a person hits this office, it often means there's some separating which hasn't been done. It's creating depression, because the self wants to 'be,' it wants to emerge. It just doesn't want to stay inside any longer."

Even healthy adults occasionally have encounters with parents that leave us feeling edgy, defensive, or longing for something intangible, serving to remind us that we haven't quite closed the book on individuation and separation. We tend to trivialize these fleeting feelings of discomfort, guilt, doubt, or anxiety. We rationalize them away. But rest assuredly, they'll be back to haunt us when our last parent dies.

Dependency: Healthy Versus Unhealthy

As midlife adults, how dependent are we really on our parents? We don't think to ask ourselves this question except in retrospect, once parents are gone. The answer lies, in part, in the nature of the parent/child relationship, which continues to reshape itself as both age. We see the depth of the attachment when we meet adults who continue to talk about their parents decades after their deaths. During the years I worked as development director for a retirement home, I frequently heard residents in their seventies and eighties remark, "My mother always said . . ." or "My father taught me how to do that." Although long gone, Mom and Dad are never too far away.

The other part of the answer to this midlife puzzle lies in our understanding of the notion of "dependency." Mired in negative connotations, dependency has gotten a bad rap, especially in light of the past decade's focus on issues of "codependency." Conventional wisdom says that if we're dependent, we must be needy. Conversely, if we're needy, we can't be independent. Isn't that the crux of adolescent rebellion and struggle? But as we amble into adulthood, we learn that being independent and being dependent aren't necessarily mutually exclusive. In fact, we discover that perhaps some dependency isn't so bad. We learn that when parenting means more than meeting survival needs, a more significant bond endures.

Reuben, the father of two adult children, observes, "I watch our daughter who, at eighteen, was ready to move out to get her own place. She did all of those things—married, divorced, remarried, and had children—and still she comes over so I can balance her checkbook. And my son is this big husky bruiser of a guy who's married with three kids and can do virtually anything. But every now and then, the truck will pull up and he'll come in and say, 'I need to talk.' They couldn't have done that when they were still children. Now it's okay. Maybe the difference is that the dependence we feel when we're young, is 'Not only am I dependent, I have to do what I'm told.' When we're older, it's okay to be dependent and rely on our parents because we don't have to. I can listen and I can decide, 'No, I'm not going to do that.' I think we grow and mature in our perspective on that. And we do decide that we're all dependent throughout our lives on somebody and maybe that's not so bad."

Adult children of today have parents around for a long time. In fact, the intergenerational tie lasts longer than ever before— the lives of parents and children now commonly overlap by fifty years or more.[24] It stands to reason that for many midlife adults, parents function as the stabilizing force. We live through marriages, divorces, child rearing, career moves, job transfers—all the usual and stressful changes of midlife. But whatever we experience and however our lives change, our parents are there, like understudies waiting backstage for the moment they might be called to service.

As George expresses it, "I just knew my parents were always there. I knew that if I wanted to call them and discuss a problem, my mother would give me three hundred reasons why I should or should not do something. Or my father would say, 'Oh, don't worry about it, just go do it.' They were dependable, as a point of reference."

Even when our parents have not been dependable, they are still perceived as parents as long as they live. They may be "do as I say, not as I do" parents. They may be emotionally distant or perhaps they smother us. No matter, they are our parents. And as we have seen, despite our ambivalence and tangled feelings, we mourn their loss.

The Unique Relationship

So what is it about the parent/child relationship that makes it so unique, so enduring? Lillian Troll, in *Families in Later Life*, describes it as a relationship that transcends geographic, socioeconomic, and developmental changes in a way no other relationship does.[25] In these shifting economic times, it's not unusual for job transfers to separate families by thousands of miles but most of us continue to maintain regular contact with our parents. Visits may be infrequent, but technology—such as e-mail, beepers, cell phones, and home video—enables us to connect with an immediacy that is historically unprecedented.

Regardless of the nature of our relationship with our parents, we don't sever our ties with them at anywhere near the rate at which we untie the marital knot. We may replace our partner but parents are constant, even if *they* have divorced a number of times. When adult children end a marriage, many find themselves turning to Mom and Dad for support for the first time in decades. While research does not yield any definitive answers about the difference between married and divorced children in response to parental death, it is likely that divorced adult children have more contact and receive more assistance from parents and, thus, may have a more difficult time when they lose parents.

For a time, I questioned whether the depth of my own reaction to my parents' deaths was exacerbated by my divorce, which drew me closer to my parents in their last years. After all, it was my divorce that presented the greatest trial of my relationship with my parents. As I dealt with a floundering marriage, my folks were experiencing dramatic upheavals in their lives—the diagnosis of my father's Alzheimer's disease and the deaths of my mother's sister and her husband. Our relationship was tested by events that altered our lives and the family dynamic significantly, but that original connection, which teetered perilously at times, managed to survive. Our struggles, as seemingly disparate as they were, pulled us together with binds that held tighter than ever before. In lighter moments, I viewed it as a case of "misery loves company." In more introspective times, I understood that, ultimately, a lifetime of love and gratitude on both sides had come home to roost.

It is probably much easier and far more satisfying to recite what we gave our parents in their later years than it is to explain what it is that we got from them. What is it exactly that we, as adult children, expect from our parents and precisely how does parental support change through the years? According to one study, adult children appear to receive the greatest support during the period of a first marriage and the establishment of a family, with the most common form of assistance being counseling and advice.[26] Apparently, the characteristics of the parents rather than those of the child are more strongly associated with giving assistance. Parents in good health are more likely to give various types of assistance, whereas divorced or widowed parents are less likely to provide help, largely due to reduced financial station. Widowed and divorced parents may also have less emotional reserves. On the other hand, they may now develop active social lives that preclude giving as much time to their children as before their circumstances changed.

One study found there was considerable agreement among adult children and parents that one of the most important aspects of the filial role is to provide affection and emotional support. Over half of adult children reported feeling that their parents were a potential as well as an actual source of assistance; until their midforties most adult children saw their parents as someone on whom they could call for financial or emotional help.[27]

As adults, we continued to see our parents as the ballast. As the years progressed, we provided more and more support for them. We acted as sounding boards, cheered them in their depression, and listened to their fears and concerns. Some of us served our folks by chauffeuring, shopping, or taking care of their bills or their medical care. We helped arrange care for them. Many times, we have come to their aid financially, even when it strained our budgets.

Did we do enough for our aging parents? That's a question that sometimes plagues us after they're gone. No matter how much we do for our parents, somehow we still manage to feel guilty, even when they don't impose it on us. Guilty if we don't call or visit enough. Guilty if we place them in a nursing home, guilty if we take them into our own home and then resent the responsibility. One study suggests that children's pervasive guilt in regard to parent care may be a reflection of the personal myth that they cannot meet their parent's dependency needs in the same way the parent met their own needs in childhood.[28] It's worth noting here that research indicates that sons and daughters express similar attitudes toward providing for their parents but daughters are much more likely than sons to actually provide the care.[29]

It isn't until we are able to see our parents as individuals who may require assistance but who continue to have their own needs and rights that we reach a level of healthy filial maturity. So exactly who is dependent upon whom in the later years? It's significant that in a study of parents' and adult children's attitudes on caretaking, both groups perceived role reversal—with the child taking care of the parent—as a dysfunctional perception of the filial role. With today's increasingly mobile society, it's simply not that common for children and parents to live in close proximity to each other. Caretaking often involves making long-distance alternative arrangements.

What is fascinating in these studies is the apparent discrepancy between the expectancies of older people with regard to assistance from their children and what adult children feel they should provide to their older parents.[30] One significant study found that the majority of the oldest generation but only a minority of other generations felt that professional services could replace some family-provided services. In other words, older generations would rather pay professionals for assistance than ask family members.[31] More than likely, these parents value their independence and don't wish to become a burden on their children.

Of course, what our parents wanted and what actually happened in the end are not always one and the same. No one counts on being debilitated. We would all like to die without prolonged illness or physical deterioration, or, as an elderly blues musician once told me, "Everybody wanna go to heaven but nobody wanna die." More often than not, the road to heaven is not a scenic one. And so we are left with memories of parents whose last years may have been far from golden. For us, the surviving adults, the task is to shelve those unhappy final memories and to pull out the stories that help us recall lovingly who our parents were.

Resolving Our Issues Through Memories

Everyone I interviewed had stories to tell—funny anecdotes, sad tales, and family tidbits that have continued to nourish our souls. Talking about our parents allows us to maintain connections with them. We keep the memories alive and we integrate them into the present and into our relationships with others, fashioning a story that seems "right." We work on our relationship with our deceased parents, like working on a jigsaw puzzle, in hopes that unresolved issues might get resolved. The process of sharing our memories can crystallize the identity of a parent, helping to work out the relationship.[32]

John Bradshaw, whose work has brought hope and a new lease on life to millions of adult children of dysfunctional families, notes that these adults have a terrific need to figure things out because their parents were unpredictable adult children themselves. Of this parenting, Bradshaw writes, "Sometimes they parented you as adults; sometimes they parented you as wounded and selfish children. Sometimes they were in *their* addictions, sometimes not. What resulted was confusion and unpredictability." And, as Bradshaw says, "until you heal the past, you will continue to try to figure it out."[33]

Many of us attempt to resolve our relationships with our parents while they are living, obviously the preferred modus operandi. In the heartwarming movie *Mother,* John Henderson (played by Albert Brooks) is a twice-divorced professional writer with a bad case of writer's block. He returns to his childhood home to live with his mother for a time. He believes that their relationship is the root of not only his failed marriages but his present dilemma as well. In the process of reworking his relationship with her, Henderson learns about his mother's thwarted hopes and dreams, forges a new, more honest, and, ultimately, loving relationship with her, and finds his way back to his true self.

But *Mother* is a movie. Just as it has a storybook ending with the promise of a new romance for Henderson, we always hope that if we can resolve our relationship with our parents, our life will change for the better. And it would, if only we could do it successfully. That, unfortunately, is not so easily accomplished.

FATHERS AND MOTHERS

Who Were They?

ne day while driving, I tuned in to *Dr. Laura's Show,* the syndicated radio program hosted by psychologist Laura Schlessinger. A young man called in, distressed because his wife refused to give up her full-time job to stay home with their three-year-old son. This obviously concerned father felt that the early formative years were most important to their son's healthy development. He was committed to making the sacrifices that the loss of his wife's salary would ensue, but he was unable to persuade her to give up her job. He wanted Dr. Laura's help in figuring out how to reach his wife. When Dr. Laura suggested that he quit *his* job to stay home with his son for a few years, the young father was speechless. At first, he seemed to think that Dr. Laura had misunderstood and he attempted to rephrase his question to get the support he wanted. When he finally got it, his sincere response was that he had always believed that he was most valuable to his family in the workforce. Dr. Laura pointed out that by subscribing to that notion, he was devaluing his worth as a parent. The man acknowledged that this had never occurred to him and he would have to give it consideration. A novel idea, indeed!

Developmental theories have always focused on the mother's role as primary caregiver but in fact, with economic, social, and other factors changing this norm, fathers are increasingly taking more responsibility for their children. What's more, they are discovering that they can do a fine job. In *The Courage to Raise Good Men*, authors Olga Silverstein and Beth Rashbaum refer to the collapse of the breadwinner ethos.[34] It may be that Father as sole breadwinner (and subsequently, hero) is no longer the norm, but for most midlife orphans who grew up in the fifties, Father fulfilled a traditional role in the family. He was the patriarch who earned most of the income and connected to his children largely according to behavior that was dictated by society's standards. Whether Father's role was more disciplinarian, buddy, or mentor depended somewhat upon his individual personality but more often on his preconceived notion of his role in the family, which was, to a great degree, an outgrowth of his relationship with his own father.

Longing for Father

If mothers provide the pillar and the security for the family, fathers (traditional or otherwise) also have their place. Fathers encourage independence and individuation. Were it not for Dad's intervention, it might be more difficult to sustain a healthy separation from Mom. A father is a model of masculinity for his son. And who's the first man to tell a young girl how beautiful she is? With his praise, Dad confirms his daughter's femininity. Father provides a second fount of unwavering love, so mother isn't left being the sole source. It's okay to be mad at Mom when we have Dad. And, as Judith Viorst writes, "if we have no father, we will long for him."[35]

That's how it was for Delia, whose father died when she was ten. She describes her reaction as "someone opened up the floor underneath me." This was the man she adored, whose job took him abroad for long stretches. Each time he returned, Delia recalls, she made a flying leap into his arms. He'd take out the atlas and point out the places he had been and entertain her with stories of his travels. She remembers that once he read her (in German) a book about climbing Mt. Everest, translating patiently. She recalls details like the fact that he always smoked a couple of cigarettes or a pipe after dinner or how he played the violin with her mother accompanying on piano. Although her father was not in her life for very long and was away for a good deal of that time, Delia's memories of him as the hero and protector are vivid.

Not surprisingly, Delia's first husband didn't measure up to her idea of what a husband should be. She describes him as very dependent, almost childlike, but one wonders whether he ever had a chance. In her second marriage, however, Delia's expectations were more realistic. In this relationship, she has been able to indulge the love of adventure that she inherited from her father. She and her husband share an interest in scuba diving, which takes them on travels around the world. Delia's sister, a freelance international photographer, has made a career out of her similar love of travel.

When we are fortunate enough to have had a good father, we don't have to wonder who he was and what he was about—we know. But for those not as lucky, for instance, those who had emotionally distant or impaired fathers, the longing may be as intense as if there had been no father, as it is for Seth.

Although Seth's memories of his parents are an amalgam of

good and bad, his lingering grief is largely about his relationship with his father. His father's alcoholism was a problem for as long as Seth can remember, and the family always had money problems. "We would regularly have utilities turned off and Sheriff Sale signs on the house. There were nine kids so it wasn't easy."

Seth recalls how much fun his father could be, an affable man with an engaging personality who attracted lots of friends. He often brought strangers home and offered them the couch. When Seth was young, theirs was a very sociable home, a lively place to be in many ways. But there was a dark side that the family tried to hide. Both parents drank heavily. Seth's father tended to keep his thoughts to himself and would become withdrawn until he would fly into an alcoholic rage, verbally abusing his wife and children. In one awful scene that Seth has never forgotten, his drunken father brought a girlfriend home and Seth's mother kicked him out. His parents had terrible arguments, and, several times over the years, they separated. Finally, when most of their children were grown, they both entered a rehab and together recovered from their alcoholism. Although the family pulled together in the last few years, the damage of those early years was done.

Seth wipes away tears as he speaks of his father's death several years earlier. "I didn't have a lot of respect for my dad. He would get into arguments with me and my brothers and sisters, and often there were physical confrontations. It was hard for me to lose him because things were not finished even though he had recovered. I knew that he would never [choking up] . . . I knew when he died that I wasn't going to have the opportunity to work things out with him. It was the end of the hope for that to happen and that was the hardest thing for me."

George also grew up with an alcoholic father. But his memories are vastly different from Seth's because his father, despite his illness, managed to be there for his son. When George speaks of his parents, it is with a tender, almost bemused air. Carefully balancing a tray of plump strawberries, creamy cheese spreads, and fresh bakery bread on one of the speakers in his crowded home music studio, George obviously relishes this opportunity to talk.

"My dad was very laid-back. He was really just a 'take it as it goes' kind of a guy. He was really the artist in the family. My mother had a lot of artistic qualities, and she intellectually understood art, but my father was the artist. He was a builder and really an architectural artist. He knew beauty. He could create beauty out of bricks and mortar. My father learned from his father, who had learned from his father. That's where I get pride in doing that kind of work. When you learn from your own parent, you learn to do something well. Then there's only one way to do it, which is the correct way." Smiling, George asks me, "You know what I mean?"

He continues, "My parents were teachers—Mom taught high school and my father was a builder and taught in a vocational school. My father was home by five-thirty every night, so we always had dinner together. When he was sober, he was fine, a regular dad. I would always talk to him when he was sober. My father's alcoholism increased during our teenage years but after I left to go away to high school on a music scholarship, my father went back to school and got his master's degree. Each of my parents was the youngest child in their families so they were used to having everything their way, two spoiled brats. That probably led to some of their difficulties. My mother used to nag him terribly, she always wanted him to be something more. When I was in college, they finally separated. But Dad still came to the house all the time and repaired things. He was always around."

As George reminisces, he chuckles frequently, painting a veneer that almost glosses over another part of the unfolding story.

"I was a very sensitive kid and very emotional. I didn't think my father treated my mother very well. I'd ask her, 'Why don't you just get rid of him, just divorce him?' and she'd say, 'He's just sick, you know.' I think I probably had the worst reaction of anybody in the whole house. I was probably the most upset by these alcoholic episodes. I must have loved my dad before all this stuff started, so I was probably really mad at him. I didn't hold it in. I was kind of hyper, all over the place."

George pauses for a moment and then concludes, "After you're older you understand what's going on. Back then, I was seeing through the eyes of a child. But now as an adult, and realizing how hard it is to be married to somebody under the best of circumstances, I can see that it must have been an awesome task for my mother. Mom had the additional burden of an alcoholic spouse and an aging parent all in the same house with two children. Talk about a Pandora's box. Wow. She really had a lot on her hands."

For some adult children, it's only after parents are gone that we can assess fairly the people who meant so much to us but who were not capable of giving us what we needed. It's only when we can see them as individuals with frailties as well as strengths that we can finally accept them—and our own flawed selves as well. For Will, a midlife orphan, insights into his father are helping rid himself of destructive behavior that has plagued him for most of his life.

Will is a vigorously handsome man, a talented musician, and a historian with an outgoing personality and a penchant for storytelling. A recovering alcoholic, he has been divorced three times and his children are grown. The impeccably furnished Victorian home that he shares with his significant other reflects their many intellectual and artistic pursuits. Will begins the interview by explaining that his father was in the Navy and away a lot when he and his brother were young.

"My mom was definitely in charge but when he was home, she deferred to him to discipline us. I can remember that he spanked me once and I refused to cry so he said, "Okay, I won't spank you anymore." I had to respect him for that. And another time, he told me to write an essay when I lied about something. I thought that was great because it taught me to think about the consequences of what I'd done. When I was about fourteen, he left my mother for another woman. I was very angry with him. Nobody was divorced in those days, it was unheard of in the fifties. But he was a flamboyant, radical leftist, a very artistic man, and my mother was socially conservative, kind of Victorian almost. They were totally mismatched."

After the divorce, Will's relationship with his father grew distant. It wasn't until he was in college that they reconnected. After they spent a glorious day sailing together, an activity they had shared when Will was young, Will decided to let go of his tremendous anger. That summer, he lived with his father and stepmother and further cemented the relationship. However, Will continued to struggle with the emotions borne of his insecure childhood and his missing father. He says now, "I feel some guilt and regret that I wasn't there at the end for my father. At the time he got sick, I was drinking heavily and in the midst of my second divorce. I went through some bad times."

Will continues, "I've stopped drinking now and turned my life around. My father was always proud of my accomplishments so I was sorry he didn't live to see my first book published. I celebrate his life, which was so rich. I didn't fully appreciate how neat a man he was—he was a frustrated actor, active in community theater, and he wrote plays. He was always good with his hands. When I was about nine or ten, he converted a ten-foot rowboat into a sailboat completely by hand. We sailed it together to the middle of the Long Island Sound and back, a whole day's trip. I've never forgotten it. I kept those wooden hoops he made for the sails and I used to hang my flutes on them. I still keep his compass in my car."

Will is able to see his father for the man he was. He's learning to look at himself in light of the man who disappointed him when he was young. Perhaps Will can now find the peace in a stable relationship that thus far has eluded him. The constructive changes he has made at work have not gone unnoticed. At this point in his life, he is more content than ever before and is taking good care of himself.

For some adults, Father was "missing in action," either physically or emotionally absent. For the more fortunate, Dad provided what Mom, often more cautious and protective, did not—a more carefree or adventurous approach to life, encouraging us to challenge ourselves to physical feats. Father tossed us high in the air as infants and rode with us on the tallest ferris wheel. Father drove faster and farther than Mother. Mother said "Be careful" when we played on the rocks by the water and Father took our hand and helped us cross. Mother was about security. Father was about risk.

Describing the difference between her parents, Bess says, " My mother was more intense; she tended to be a worrier. I used to tell her that she would wake up worrying in the morning and then look for something to attach it to. Dad was more adventurous and easygoing. When I was in high school and stayed out real late—usually just at someone's house watching *Inner Sanctum* or something like that—my mom used to walk the floor until I came in. One night I was really late, so she sent my father to find me. He drove by the house where I said I'd be. We were all out on my friend's porch. Dad just drove by and waved to me. It wasn't until later that I realized he was out looking for me."

Bess's father combined his sense of responsibility toward his child with an instinctual respect for her adolescent autonomy. It's for that sensitivity to her needs and his constant presence in her life that Bess is most grateful.

Even though it was not in Phil's father's nature to exactly let loose, his attempts at bonding earned this rather starchy father respect from his son. Despite the fact that his father was "stern, formal, and a strict disciplinarian," as Phil describes him, he routinely tried to make time for his son.

Phil offers me a glass of red wine as we relax in the elegant living room of the house he shares with his second wife. With his dark hair neatly clipped, Phil is dressed casually but impeccably in a navy crewneck sweater and pressed pants, looking much like an adult version of a prep school boy.

He speaks wistfully of his father. "He liked baseball and I loved it so we used to go outside and have catches. In the summer, he'd take me to see the professional teams play—that was always fun. He was a traveling salesman and on the road a lot so I wasn't particularly close with him, but I loved him. I don't remember having father-son chats about anything. He was very stern and too formal for that—it wasn't unusual for him to sit around the house with his tie on. Over the years, he mellowed. As I got older and more financially sound, he accepted me more as an adult. It wasn't a warm, fuzzy relationship but it was a nice one. After my mother got sick, he wanted me to come visit frequently and he seemed to really enjoy our visits. When he was dying, I sat by his bed for hours. Sometimes we barely spoke because he was so weak but the nurse would always tell me how much he said he liked my being there."

Phil acknowledges that his involvement with his own children from his first marriage was probably modeled after his father's parenting. He regrets that he wasn't more available to them. He describes himself as somewhat reticent and aloof but closer with his children than his father was with him. He has been much more present and active in raising his daughter from his second marriage. Phil was surprised to see his father's response to grandchildren—he was doting and affectionate. "It was like he knew how to do it now and he was going to do it right."

Men and Their Fathers

For Derek, memories of his father, with whom he worked in the family business, are filled with rage, confusion, and guilt, as well as love. He describes their relationship as so neurotic that Derek was unable to figure out what it was that he wanted out of life until he finally liquidated the business when his father became infirm. Yet it was his father whom Derek continued to mourn even after his mother, his last parent, died.

"My father was a passive husband and father. He basically abdicated his responsibility by throwing us at the mercy of my mother, who was severely pathological. It was difficult for me to have any personal growth because, for twenty-five years, my father was my boss. I loved him with a kind of neurotic love, loved him so much that I injured myself to buoy him up. I was always worried that something would happen to him, because he was always saying, 'It's a hard world.' I felt that to surpass him would be tantamount to killing him. I could only live under his shadow. So when I finally liquidated the business, I had to figure out what to do with my life."

After dabbling successfully in the stock market for a number of years, Derek went back to school and became a clinical psychologist. At fifty-eight, he has a thriving practice. He's tremendously enthusiastic about his work and proud of his home and family.

"My father would turn over in his grave if he could see how nice I have it. I think if I hadn't been in analysis, I probably wouldn't have picked the right woman or made some of the good decisions I did. I've struggled over issues with my own son. What I did was hard, taking care of myself was very hard because of my sense of love and loyalty to my father."

Derek had to separate from his father in order to survive. He did it while his father was still living by getting out of the business but now he continues to wrestle with his guilt. He sees himself in those former days as a man who carried around the attitude of a little boy. With a wry smile, he remarks, "If we could just say 'Grow up' it would be so much easier, but it doesn't happen that way."

At the other extreme was Jay's experience with his father, a hardworking man dedicated to his family, a value borne of immigrant parents who gave up everything to move from Europe to Wisconsin, where their children would have opportunity.

Jay recalls, "When I'd get mad at my sister, my father would tell me not to criticize her. He'd emphasize that 'such is life' and that I should love my sister. He was awfully good at making me feel guilty. It was always, 'Don't you think I care? Don't you think I'm doing this for love?' But he always made us feel so protected and loved and he gave us so much guidance. How could you want to rebel against somebody who loves you so unequivocally with all your faults?"

Like Jay, Mark's bond with his father was strong. Mark is grateful that he was able to spend his father's last years in close proximity. After his mother died in Arizona, where his parents had been living, Mark encouraged his father to move back east. Nearing eighty years old, his dad insisted on living on his own and he did his own laundry and cooked in his apartment.

Says Mark, "He was very self-sufficient, with absolutely no limitations. He used to walk across the street to the Y and he'd swim, walk the track, and just talk to the guys. We made sure my father was a part of our life. When we had people to dinner, he was included. All of our friends knew my father and they really enjoyed him. He was very pleasant, interesting, and argumentative in a friendly kind of way. He was very aware, he'd read the papers, watch the news shows. He was up on current events and culture. He didn't have any plans for death. He thought he was going to live to be ninety or ninety-five. He once said, 'I'm just going to get more crotchety and more and more of a pain in the ass.' The one thing he really wanted to do was to visit Israel and he got a passport and made plans. He never made it," concludes Mark sadly.

Brian, whose father was ninety-four when he died, fondly recalls the fishing outings he and his father shared so often. Because Brian was born when his parents were older, his father was preparing to retire just as Brian left for college.

Brian recalls, "The interesting thing about my father was that he was originally from a rural area in Canada and he would tell me about all the changes he'd seen in one lifetime—from going outside to use the outhouse to seeing the first car and the first phone come to town. He was an engineer for the phone company and he was involved in the [installation of the] first long-distance dialing telephone. He was a very active person, always working around the house, up on ladders all the time.

"It's not like he wasn't around, he was. But he wasn't happy with my mother and he was pretty passive about her drinking and her emotional illness. As a kid, I think I felt the tension but I didn't have any siblings to compare things with. I didn't realize anything was wrong even though my parents slept in separate bedrooms. I was always more comfortable being with my father. He accepted me. I just enjoyed him. When I was older, I felt that my mother got in the way of my relationship with him.''

Brian smiles and shakes his head as he remembers a particularly sour point in his relationship with his father. "At one point when I was in my late twenties, my father got furious with me about something and he disinherited me for a while. I don't know if he actually changed his will but he was convinced I was totally out of my mind. For about five years I didn't see my parents, but we reconciled finally. I think in some ways my father always understood that the reason I wasn't there very much when he got sick was because of my mother—her alcoholism and her manipulative behavior were real problems for me."

He adds, "Clearly, I'm my father's son. A lot of the good qualities I have are his, to the extent that loyalty is important to me like it was to him. I'm very loyal to my friends and family and even to my employers. I think the sensitivity and caring that I have probably comes from my father. It's funny when I hear myself tell my girlfriend's son that education is important, it's just like my father used to say to me."

Brian's voice drops as he says, "You know, it was winter when my father died so I never really put his ashes anywhere. In the spring, I buried part of his ashes in the river where we used to fish. That's what brought his death home for me and made it real."

Daughters and Dads

I was in sixth grade when my parents had the first argument that I can remember that was directly related to me. They had taken me shopping for new dress clothes. After I picked out an outfit, I begged for a pair of matching Capezios, the soft kidskin flats that came in an array of colors and were the rage. My dad took me over to the shoe department and I tried a pair of the coveted shoes on, pirouetting in front of the mirror and dancing around my smiling father. My mother, practical and frugal, nixed the sale. "She doesn't need those. She already has dress shoes."

Furious, I began to beg and whine. When my parents started to argue with each other, I quickly shut up, mortified that I had provoked this scene. We left without the shoes. I sulked for days and directed my anger at my mother, who had overruled my father. I knew that he *would* have bought the shoes for me had it not been for her.

Years later when I was in college, my father promised that if I made Dean's List, he would buy me a car for graduation and I could pay him back half the cost once I started working. Mom was, of course, opposed to the idea on no specific grounds that I could understand. This time my father ignored my mother's objections. When I graduated, not only did he buy me the car, he later told me to forget the loan—my rent and car maintenance were enough expenses for a new graduate. I knew the car caused a rift between my parents but my father became my true champion.

Was he really? In retrospect, his extravagant gift, so out of character, was bewildering. I don't know what prompted him to risk my mother's disapproval to indulge me that time. Perhaps it was because I had always asked for so little. But what I loved more than the car was that my father, by indulging me, made me feel so special. Isn't that what fathers are for?

Donna, whose father died when she was seventeen, remembers "funny little things" about her fallen hero. "I think about my father a lot, about how he wasn't very hairy and how he loved the sun, he had the kind of skin that didn't have lots of pores. He wasn't a tyrant but he liked things orderly. He didn't like to see the washcloths hung over the faucet handles and he'd make us hang them up. Once my face broke out and he taped an article from the paper on the bathroom mirror on how to care for your skin. I remember when I was about thirteen, he tried to talk to me about the birds and bees and I thought that it was pretty odd that he should be doing it instead of my mother."

In Sheila's family, her father was the commander-in-chief. He was the handyman who fixed machines and the adviser who mended feelings. "My father was a great guy, the kind of person who always handled everything in our family. If you had a problem, you went to Dad. He wasn't the kind that would hug you and kiss you and say 'I love you,' but you always knew that he had the solution to the problem, any kind of problem," says Sheila. "When I got married, if our refrigerator broke and we weren't sure what to do about it, I could call my father and say, 'Dad, it's making a funny noise. What do you think?'

"Throughout all of his life, he had taken care of everything and then, when my mom died, I suddenly became the parent and he became the child. I would call him and he'd say, 'I was going to cook dinner and went to the freezer and I have two pork chops. What am I going to do with the other one?' He broke my heart, absolutely broke my heart when he said that."

What happens when a father wanted a son but got a daughter instead? Danielle recalls that her father, who'd always wanted a son, became a Cub Scout master. "I was the only person in the family who would go on scout outings with him. We shared a motorboat with our neighbors but, again, I was the only one who'd go out with him. My mother and sister were always out getting their hair done so I went lots of places with him and we did things together. One summer I worked for him and I remember he took me to the Playboy Club for lunch. It's funny to think about now.

"My father was full of life. He loved to gamble. My mother tried to set limits but he was horribly indulgent. My sister would carry on and the way he dealt with it was to basically give her whatever she wanted. He made a good living and he wouldn't let my mother work but I think she would have been a happier person if she could have worked."

Danielle says wistfully, "He was a great dancer. I miss dancing with him. My father would have loved my boys, especially because he always wanted a son. My younger one resembles my dad—he looks like him and has his disposition; he's more temperamental."

Jean remembers a father who parented poorly but offers that "it was the only way he knew how, it was his Russian background. I was too young to understand that he had lost all of his family in the Holocaust. He was just too dogmatic and I didn't feel a closeness to him. My sister was able to appreciate him, but for some reason I wasn't. When my mother would buy me something I wanted, she'd tell me to hide it from my father because he didn't like to spend money. After he died, I thought maybe my mother would start to live the way she should have all those years. When my father died, I had some real resentments that I couldn't work through for a long time."

For Ronni, "father" evokes memories of a man steeped in tradition, duty bound to provide the best for his family, distant and detached from his children. A very successful businessman, Ronni's father sent each of his seven children off to exclusive prep schools whether or not they wanted to go. "He was about forty when I was born and I was the sixth child. I think he had a soft heart and could be an emotional man at times but, unfortunately, mostly his leading emotion was anger. He was always dominated by the women in his life, first by my mother and then his second wife. I had a conflictual relationship with him most of my life."

Ronni's father's alcoholism, workaholism, and sexual inappropriateness make it difficult for her to make peace with his memory. At the same time, she acknowledges that her love of outdoors and athleticism comes directly from her father, who loved all kinds of sports. She concedes, however, that the attention their father gave his children for their athletic prowess was "the major incentive for excelling." For Ronni and most of her siblings, the man who was their father remains an enigma who was able to give his children everything but the love that they so craved.

Who were our fathers? They were heroes. They were villains. They were indulgent, withholding, stern, or sentimental. They were affectionate. They were aloof. They were men striving to live up to the ideals of a society that put great demands on them. They were responsible for the economic survival of their families. Some caved in under the pressure, forever affecting the lives of their children. More were constant and loving providers, sources of great strength for their families. However wonderful Father was, though, for most of us it was Mother we called for when we were sick, hurting, or needy. Mother—invincible, indestructible, and always there.

"But Most of All, I Remember Mama"

These were the words that began each episode of one of America's favorite television shows in the fifties. In this weekly drama about an immigrant Swedish family, Mama (played by Peggy Wood) was central to the resolution of each show's conflict. "Mama" was the universal mother—loving, accepting, patient, and infinitely wise.

Despite the growing number of fathers who play a central part in their children's lives, the mother figure as the foundation of the family—the rock—remains, for most people, the reality. In her introduction to *Motherless Daughters,* Hope Edelman refers to the place in our psyche where *mother* represents comfort and security no matter what our age, and where our mother/child bond is so primal that we equate its severing with a child's emotional death.[36] It's no wonder that when the last parent to die is the mother—the most common order of parental death—we may grieve even more intensely. How do we say farewell to the woman who carried us to life?

Gina, a fifty-year-old homemaker attending a seminar on personal growth, was appalled when the speaker, a nun, commented, "Just because you had a mother doesn't mean you had a good mother." Recalling those words, Gina says, "They were meant to have shock value. And for me, they did. I had a wonderful mother. I couldn't imagine otherwise."

Gina's relationship with her mother was an exceptionally good one and she has modeled her own life on the woman she so revered. "I always wanted to be here for my kids, like my mother was for us. Fortunately, we could afford that and my husband never pushed me to go out and work." Gina stayed home while she raised her children. She was their chauffeur, their cheerleader, their nurse, their confidante—the mother that her own mother had been to her. At times, she worked in her husband's office or handled paperwork for his busy medical supply business. Separated by a thousand miles, Gina and her mom spoke on the phone regularly, sometimes even more than once a day. When her mother became ill, Gina flew out and stayed with her for weeks at a time. It is no surprise to Gina that her own children are as close with her as she was with her mother.

Like Gina, Bess considered her mother her best friend. When

she was young, Bess's grandparents cared for her while her mother worked in public relations and her father worked nights as a security supervisor for a large office building. Her grandmother did the cooking and housekeeping—Bess's mother had not a whit of interest in housework. Yet, Bess says, her mother, despite her long working hours, was definitely in charge of her only child. She meted out discipline and deferred to no one. She always made time for her child, attending school plays and activities as much as possible. Bess admits that during her adolescent years, she and her mother had some turbulent times. As Bess matured, their relationship smoothed out. They even worked in the same government agency for seven years. They traveled to Europe together, visiting Paris, London, and Frankfurt. They indulged their mutual love of shopping together almost every Saturday afternoon. Her death left a gaping hole in Bess's life, which she is slowly coming to terms with.

"I miss my mother's interest in the things that I'm doing with my life," says Ray in his slight Southern twang. "She always wanted to hear what I was doing and she encouraged me to succeed and do well but also to be sure to take time and smell the roses. She was a very artsy person—she studied painting and worked with clay. She had been a teacher before she married my father. She gave it up to raise a family. But whatever she did, she worked hard at it. I think a lot of the dedication to work that I have and to putting in long hours, I got from her."

Ray becomes more agitated as he reflects on what he sees as his mother's weakness—her enabling behavior. "When I was in college, my brother, who had had all kinds of problems, got in trouble and was arrested for beating his wife while he was intoxicated. I told my parents to let him stay in jail, that they couldn't keep bailing him out of trouble, but my mother wouldn't hear of it. And my brother got worse over the years. Once when I came home, I found all these liquor bottles that my brother had hidden. When I confronted my mother about his problem, she commented that since I had never been around alcohol that much, I couldn't know what a drinking problem was. She was in complete denial where my brother was concerned. I sometimes wonder if the stress from my brother contributed to her illness."

The midlife adults I interviewed, almost without exception, were introspective individuals who have been able to acknowledge both the positive and the negative characteristics and attributes of their mothers. Perhaps that is not so surprising, since these were people who volunteered to be interviewed. However, what was surprising as well as striking was the willingness to exonerate Mother, regardless of the complicated, tangled feelings that endure.

According to Lani, whose mother's alcoholism was so bad when Lani was in middle school that she and her brother were removed from the family home, there was no need to forgive her mother. "She didn't choose to do this to any of us. Her alcoholism was a disease, like cancer. You don't have to forgive anyone for being sick with cancer. My mother and I were the only ones in my family that really talked about it later."

For Lani, "later" refers to the time after her mother came out of the rehabilitation hospital. Lani and her mother grew closer once her mother recovered, and Lani became her mother's champion. "I always felt close to my parents, even as a little girl. I didn't want to go to school, I wanted to stay home and do puzzles with my mother. My mom had this way of talking to you that made you feel better even though she never said anything that was gonna change it." Lani recalls how her mother tried to prepare her for her death. "She was so calm and peaceful and so strong. Once we were waiting at the hospital for her to have X rays and she said to me, 'If ever I can't talk, I want to have a signal with you to let you know that I can hear you and I understand you. In the palm of your hand, I'll write the letter *J*.'

"Well, I didn't want to hear it. At the end when she was dying, I leaned over to her ear real close and I said, 'Mom, I'm here, it's Lani.' With that, she turned her head and put her arm out and made the sign. I knew she knew I was there."

Not everyone can find it in his or her heart to pardon what may seem like unpardonable transgressions. Derek, who worked in his father's business, was emotionally tied to a father who was completely passive in his relationship with a woman incapable of giving her children love. He describes his mother as paranoid with low self-esteem, narcissistic, and intellectually ignorant. As a result, she didn't tolerate others and avoided contact with anyone outside the family. Theirs was a tense, unhappy home. Although Derek can sympathize that his mother lost her own mother when she was young and she and her siblings were farmed out to relatives, he cannot find it in himself to excuse her "crazy behavior that traumatized me and my siblings."

Derek lowers his voice and smirks because he is aware that his next comment is provocative: "When my mother died, we went to the funeral home. They make you walk to where the body is, across this kind of supermarket of coffins, with the prices going up as you walk. When I went to identify my mother, I took a good look at her and thought to myself, 'Is she really dead? Is she really dead?'"

Derek says he sincerely does not miss his mother, who he believes was a very emotionally destructive individual. At the time of her death, Derek was in analysis. He feels that he probably had already done some grief work while his mother was still living. He remarks that part of the reason he is so passionate about the counseling he does today is because of his experience growing up. The flip side is, according to Derek, "maybe if I were nourished, I would have been doing this years ago."

Nourishment, emotional sustenance, love, support, encouragement—the staff of life that all children want to sample. If we're lucky, our parents dole it out generously, filling our plates. If we're not as fortunate, we suffer, victims of emotional malnutrition.

Healthy Parents, Healthy Child

Salt-and-pepper curls reach to the base of Ernie's neck. At fifty-four years old, he has already retired and is enjoying his life immensely. Jeans and flannel shirts have replaced his wardrobe of dark suits and corporate ties. His skin is deeply tanned by the two weeks he and his wife have just spent vacationing in the Mediterranean. I have known them for twenty-five years and they are two of my favorite people—bright, talented, spirited, and still very much in love. Before we talk, Ernie makes me a cup of tea, shuffling back and forth between the kitchen and the family room where we are seated. Although we've shared life's vicissitudes through the years, Ernie rarely reveals his emotions and I wonder aloud if this interview will be uncomfortable for him. He assures me he is fine and begins to reminisce about his parents.

Ernie was thirty-seven when his dad, a physician, died. Although his father made a comfortable living, he wasn't, as Ernie phrased it, "a financial kind of guy." He frequently bartered his services, accepting homegrown tomatoes and peppers from his patients in lieu of payment. He had been an athlete of some prowess until a heart attack at age thirty-eight changed that. Medical opinion of the time relegated him to a physically inactive lifestyle.

He switched from sports to painting, which became a lifelong passion. His framed watercolors cover the walls of Ernie's home.

Ernie recalls that his dad took him to look at prospective colleges and that they usually managed to fit in a football game wherever they went. His death from cancer ten years ago was very difficult for Ernie, who greatly admired his father, whom he describes as "a generous and quiet man." Although he and his dad enjoyed a warm relationship, Ernie explains his and his wife's decision to move away from their parents: "We wanted to move away because our parents were both well respected in their towns. I wanted to say that what I accomplished is not because I'm my father's son, but what I did for myself."

In contrast to his dad, Ernie has always been a financial guy. Determined from a young age to retire early and enjoy the fruits of his labor, Ernie planned carefully, invested wisely, and fulfilled his dream of early retirement at fifty. His days are full and he keeps busy with his multiple interests in music, the arts, and physical challenges that have included participating in Rag Brie, the midsummer bicycle ride across the state of Iowa. Retirement gave Ernie the opportunity to care for his mother as her health deteriorated. In the last few years before she died, Ernie regularly made the six-hour ride to visit her. With his only sibling living on the other side of the country, Ernie assumed full responsibility for their mother's care.

He chats about his mother, recalling how she tutored him patiently the year he was nine, when he contracted polio and spent the year hospitalized in an iron lung. He brings out an audiotape he made of his mother reminiscing, and together we listen to her tell how she met her husband and what their life together was like. Then Ernie takes me to the basement, where he shows me hundreds of family photographs that he has yet to catalogue. He continues to speak fondly of his parents. "My mother always brought up how she didn't go to college. But she was smart, and very active in the symphony, especially organizing children's concerts. She was also active in the March of Dimes drive and she was an unpaid organist in the synagogue for eighteen years."

Ernie obviously has wonderful memories of his parents. He has carried their love and nurturing into his own marriage and family. His father's massive heart attack at a young age probably influenced his decision to retire early. He explains, "By the time most people retire, they don't have parents anymore. I would have had parents longer except that I was born when Dad was a little older. He had to go through med school and set up a practice before he could afford to have kids. When I was forty-nine, my daughter was already out of college. With only one kid, our situation was a lot different than most people's. There are so many opportunities in life but we can't always take advantage of them because we're tied to our desks and our jobs. Either you can't travel because of the kids or you're too old to appreciate it. If anything happens to me today, I'd say I've had the greatest four years [since retiring] of my life. And, let's face it, I hope I have a lot more. There's so much more I want to do."

Many of our choices are influenced either directly or indirectly by our parents and the way they lived, as was Ernie's decision to retire early. Like his well-respected father, he pursued a career that brought him success and financial security. Like his father, he indulges his artistic interests, playing jazz piano and producing plays. And although ultimately Ernie took a decidedly different route from his father, who worked until the very end of his life, he had the confidence and the drive to follow his own dream. Ernie acknowledges that his father's core values of hard work, love of people, and self-pride are instilled in him, as are his mother's drive and commitment to community. His parents' values are evident in the busy schedule that Ernie keeps in his retirement, a schedule of activities that are largely community based. Ernie is a man who is truly happy with himself and content with his life. He's grateful to parents who played a significant positive role in shaping his life.

If the main function of the family is to prepare children to assume a meaningful place in society, as posed by Barry and Phyllis Bricklin in *Strong Family, Strong Child,* then Ernie's parents succeeded.[37] One legacy of our parents' death is the task of finding a meaning to life. This may explain why such intense reflection and change occurs after the second parent dies. The death of our last parent then becomes a catalyst for growth and self-acceptance. As we recover from our loss, we begin to integrate who our parents were into who we are, psychologically picking and choosing those traits we admire and discarding those we don't. The reflection that we do when our parents die helps us to finally accept limitations—those of our parents as well as our own. At the same time, our memories and our ability to put them into perspective are what allow us to move on. And move on, we must.

STORIES OF OUR LEGACY

"Preserve your memories; they're all that's left you."

—"BOOKENDS" PAUL SIMON

The Legacy of Grandparents

*I*n the weeks leading up to Andy's Bar Mitzvah, I floated about, a buoy on a sea of anxiety. While tending to the myriad details surrounding this rite of passage, I suffered daily pangs of longing for my parents. How could we reach this awesome day without them? How desperately Mom had wanted to live to see her youngest grandchild become a Bar Mitzvah.

The stress of such a significant life event was exacerbated by my ex-husband's wedding six weeks before the Bar Mitzvah. Now, my already heightened sense of loss was compounded by another set of chaotic feelings, and the boys and I had little time to prepare for this enormous change. Almost overnight, the boys were expected to embrace an entirely new family and to affably share their father with the three younger stepbrothers who would soon be living with him. With what seemed to me extraordinary grace and good humor, Dan and Andy gave it their all—that is, until the subject of how to address their stepmother's parents arose. When the boys were told to address their stepmother's parents as "Bubbi and Pops," the names their stepbrothers used to address their grandparents, they protested. These were not *their* grandparents. It wasn't personal. It had nothing to do with *who* these people were. More than likely, the gesture was meant to welcome Dan and Andy into this new family. But it didn't feel right for them. Not yet. And so they balked. Frankly, so did I.

To me (heavyhearted that my parents wouldn't be here for the Bar Mitzvah), this whole idea of imposing a term of endearment for these instant grandparents felt like an incredible affront. It was no less so for my sons, particularly for Andy, who had been so attached to my mother. When my father was dying, Andy was the one who sat by the bedside, holding his grandfather's frail outstretched hand, undaunted by the array of wires and tubes. Andy wasn't ready to greet these new people in his life in such a familiar way. Neither was Dan, who passively resisted by simply not addressing them directly. I wasn't quite ready to hear my kids refer to relative stangers as their grandparents—it was enough just getting accustomed to the idea of them having a stepmother. Besides, the boys still had a set of grandparents whom they loved very much. Why all the pressure so soon and at such a stressful time, I wondered? There would be plenty of time to adjust. While the kids raged aloud to me, I raged silently, "Grandparents don't just happen. Grandparents are history, they're part of a legacy."

And indeed, our relationship with our grandparents is very special, one that's nurtured from the time we are born. *Bubbi* and *Pops* don't just appear on the scene. They're part of a legacy, an inheritance of love. And when we lose our parents, our children lose something that is very precious. Just as we have lost a part of our childhood when our last parent dies, so have our children lost a piece of their history. Children need time to mourn that loss so that they can later carry the legacy of their grandparents with them into their own families someday.

And so, in the weeks before the Bar Mitzvah, as the boys continued to protest this newly imposed relationship, my reaction was to bolster the legacy of my parents. I reminded Andy of how proud they would have been. I told the boys how my father was never given the opportunity to become a Bar Mitzvah but that he learned to read Hebrew later in life and loved to go to synagogue. I recalled how mortified I used to be by his loud, enthusiastic singing.

During those weeks, the kids asked me a lot about their grandparents. Unfortunately, although they had known him before, they remembered their grandfather only after he was in an advanced stage of Alzheimer's. I showed Dan my favorite photo (now hanging in our hallway) of Dad, wearing Dan's favorite cowboy hat, holding up his toddler grandson so that they were practically nose to nose. I told him how much his grandfather had loved him, how he used to hold him for hours and croon to him when he was an infant, how he changed his diapers all the time and fed him his first solid food—chocolate ice cream—over my protestations.

The closer we got to the Bar Mitzvah, the more sensitive I became. Each time Andy said how much he was going to miss Mom-mom that day, I'd begin to cry. "She'll be with us in spirit" was my halfhearted response. On the morning of his Bar Mitzvah, as he waited to approach the pulpit, Andy nudged me and pointed to the sliver of space between us and whispered, "Mom-mom's right here." I looked at my younger son, that beloved man-child of mine, and there, captured on his beaming face, was my mother's smile. I felt myself relax finally and, as if on cue, Dan squeezed my hand. Surrounded by my two loving, sensitive sons,

I felt the enormity of the legacy my parents had handed down. This ability to care and to be empathetic to others, this was what my parents had given me and, whether or not they were still here on earth, this part of their spirit lived in my children.

Perhaps that was the moment I finished my active grieving. It's hard to say if such a thing really happens. While I can't actually call it an epiphany, the Bar Mitzvah was a turning point for me. I realized, quite simply, I had had enough grieving. At last I was able to shift my preoccupation with what I had lost to what I had gained. I was ready to examine my legacy.

The personal growth that occurs after the death of parents is largely a result of how we selectively merge our parental legacy into our own value system. What we choose to accept or reject for our personal story determines who we will be without parents. The contemplation and intense personal scrutiny that follows our parents' deaths tend to alter our identity—we are transformed, becoming much less our parents and much more our own selves. We may reject our parents' religious practices, something we couldn't have done easily while they were living. Some of us find relationships that we previously might have rejected because of parental disapproval. On the other hand, we may decide to take over Dad's dry cleaning business or develop an affinity for the classical music that our parents loved. Once we can realistically assess our relationship with our parents, we will be able to draw on their strengths and discount their weaknesses. This assessment releases energy that allows us to enjoy our lives in more satisfying ways. And with that release, we are, at last, able to appreciate our legacy.

To some adults, a legacy means material possessions or money, but most of us understand that our parents' legacy is far more intangible and complex—an ethical and spiritual philosophy, a set of values, aesthetic appreciation, or simply genetic links. Their legacy is visible in our talents, skills, interests, and dislikes and more, in our skin, our eyes, and even the way we walk.

We stop looking back with longing and instead begin to examine who we are now—minus parents—and where we're heading. It's midlife crisis, in-your-face and at warp speed. Altered indelibly by the loss of our parents, we have grown up. And with that growth, we begin to assess our legacy, the inheritance that goes beyond money and possessions. We sift through the legacy of values, memories, and traditions. More than ever before, we now see, with each glimpse in the mirror or glance at our children's faces, the genetic links to our parents. We are like them in so many ways. The similarities simultaneously comfort and dismay us.

It shouldn't come as a surprise that of the midlife orphans I interviewed, those who seemed truly content and fulfilled were those who had the most positive things to say about their parents. Midlife adults like Ernie and Gina, who described growing up in happy, loving households, have found peace and contentment in their adult lives. A steady diet of love and emotional nourishment breeds individuals who can nurture others. Those who are happily engaged in life have generally been readily groomed by their parents.

Individual stories offer us insight into how midlife adults view the legacies that their parents have bequeathed. Only in the first story have I used actual names, for theirs is a story that has received public notice.

Serving Humanity

Sig Van Raan, psychologist and a midlife orphan, lives on Martha's Vineyard, off the coast of Massachusetts. Sig's parents immigrated to this country from Holland, traumatized by the horror of the Nazi occupation and politically disenfranchised in the aftermath. In contrast to the baser nature of man they observed, the Van Raans' actions during the war were a testimonial to the best of the human spirit. I repeat their story here because it is extraordinary and because the stunning legacy that the Van Raans left their son and daughters is worthy of consideration.

Ger and Gerard Van Raan were in their midtwenties when Hitler's forces swept through Amsterdam, where they lived. Passionately committed to social justice and imbued with the idealism of youth, the young couple quickly found a home in the Dutch Resistance. With their friends and compatriots, they participated in a daring assault in which they set fire to an administrative building that housed Nazi records of all the Jews in Amsterdam. Several of their cohorts were captured and executed for their role in the mission but, luckily, the couple's movements went undetected. Having escaped, they found other ways to fight the injustices they witnessed. Over the next couple of years, for varying lengths of time, the Van Raans sheltered three Jewish children in their home, at great risk to themselves. They also attempted to protect Sigmund Boedrukker, a close Jewish friend and resistance worker.

Sig, the only son of Ger and Gerard, recalls the story of his namesake, a tale he heard frequently while growing up. "My father had given his identity papers to Boedrukker in case he was questioned by the police. On the day that the authorities finally detained him, Boedrukker realized they knew his true identity. Rather than implicate my father, he managed to dispose of the incriminating papers." Sigmund Boedrukker was never seen again. The Van Raans named their only son for the man they risked their lives for and whom they considered a hero.

In 1985, the Van Raans were honored for their bravery and aid to Jews by the Holocaust Memorial Commission at a gathering for Righteous Gentiles in Washington, D.C. Their son remarks, "I still get emotional when I think of the simple act of courage that both of them committed themselves to in taking in those children. Whenever they talked about it, they talked about it with great humility. They wished they had done more. They didn't see it as an act of heroism—it was simply something that needed to be done. Both of my parents described themselves as apolitical and nonreligious but they subscribed to true Christian ideals, integrating sound humanistic passivism with Christian values."

Ger Van Raan died in the spring of 1997, five years after her husband. Sig is eloquent as he regards the legacy of his parents. "The life I've chosen in the mental health field, particularly working with young people, children, and families, is a direct reflection of the influence of my parents for doing service. They both became true models of the idea of providing service to try to make a better world. I truly feel very privileged that I have a life that allows me to take care of people."

Van Raan's parents' practice of serving the community didn't end when they left Holland. In 1963, while Sig was in college, his mother was a volunteer nurse for a foster care agency. She and her husband decided to take in two foster infants, subsequently adopting them. His parents' altruism was not always welcomed or appreciated by their two natural children and Sig was initially bothered by the adoption. But anger turned to devotion when he held the babies in his arms. As they grew up, the girls idolized their much older brother and, as Sig now says, "it was fun to be their hero figure."

Van Raan goes on to speak of an anguished young adolescent male client of his, whose father is dead and whose mother has a drug and alcohol problem. He remarks that he wishes he could thank the boy for letting him feel good about helping. In Van Raan's words, "I see myself being a father figure for this kid—

it's a transference of feelings that are so primary and primitive. In many ways, my parents gave me permission to do that. There's a tremendous sense of reward for me."

Although Sig recognized the remarkable courage of his parents while they were still alive, he was not able to fully appreciate the richness of the legacy until after his mother's death. For while they were heroes to many, Ger and Gerard were also human. For their son, the reality of his parents tarnished the luster of the myth that surrounded them. His parents' passion and commitment had a dark side, perhaps the result of their disillusion and disappointment with a world that failed to embrace all of its children. Growing up with his parents was an almost paradoxical experience for Sig. On the one hand, he found it fascinating to engage in the intellectual and political philosophical discussions that were a staple in the household. "I think they were truly honest in what they believed. I got a true celebration of life, a sense of true social justice, and strong convictions," he comments. On the other hand, their frequent somber periods were draining. Of his parents, Van Raan recalls, "What I saw growing up in America was almost contradictory. On the one hand, they were people who lived life fully, loved to have parties and celebrated the arts. But there were times when I would experience those dark, gloomy states in both of my parents. My mother was sad and depressed and it was the same with my father, far more than you would normally think."

When his father died, Sig grieved long and hard. When his mother died, Sig, though deeply saddened, was relieved that he wouldn't have to put her in a nursing home, something he had dreaded. Initially, he experienced such a tangled web of feelings that for a time, it was difficult to appreciate the legacy of his parents.

One year later, Sig is able to comment, "I think my sense of legacy is different now. A year has passed and I can be more unbiased. I can glorify my mother now without thinking about all the other stuff. It wasn't always easy to do that. I was much more emotional when my father died. I felt guilty that I wasn't more involved with him during his last year. I had gone to visit but it never felt like enough. As a man, I identified with his anger and frustration—there was more a sense of seeing myself in him. He was the kinder and more compassionate one. My mother was more demanding and critical."

Sig Van Raan is well aware that his parents, despite their short-comings, were extraordinary human beings. It is important for him that their lives become part of their grandchildren's legacy. Sig illustrates this: "About two weeks before my mother died, I took my two younger kids to see her on her birthday. Rudy, one of the Jewish boys who my parents hid, had come to visit and brought photos of his children and grandchildren. I introduced him to my kids as my 'older war brother.' I mean, how do you explain the Nazis to a six-year-old? I told my daughter about how my parents hid Rudy in their home when he seven, and she was profoundly moved by the story."

This family legacy of compassion and service to others is a gift that will continue to thrive as the memories are nurtured. A proud and loving son is determined that his parents' values, which are so deeply inculcated in himself, will become part of the texture of his children's lives.

An Appreciation for Beauty

Jill's mother wrote her this letter in September 1996, two weeks before her death.

Dear Jill,

I've felt leave takings are usually sad but when you left, I felt I was being caressed by an overflowing river of love. It's nice lying here in bed enjoying that delicious feeling. Your giving was boundless and I appreciated it beyond words. We may not see each other again but we will always be in each other's loving thoughts and memories. I have been blessed having you and Simon for children. Our relationship is treasured too because it took such a long time in coming but it did come and I'm grateful. It's the best going away present I could ever really have.

Love, Mom

When Jill shared this moving letter with me, she said it was the first time she had been able to read it without crying. As I dabbed at my own tears, I could certainly understand. What a priceless gift this mother left—a legacy of validation and affirmation of her love and respect for her children.

On their mother's headstone, a quote from Matisse illustrates what Jill and her brother define as their mother's special gift to them, her love of the beauty in nature. It reads, "Take joy in the flowers, they are there for everyone who wants to see them."

The most prized legacy that we get from our parents is not the grand piano or the diamonds or the family china. The intangible legacy is what the adults I interviewed credited their parents with—legacies that included the love of nature or of beauty, of music, of family, or the appreciation for finer things like cuisine, art, or travel. What our parents passed down to us is a way of looking at the world, a gateway to finding whatever it is that touches our souls.

My parents, neither particularly athletic or artistic, nevertheless managed to pass on to me an appreciation for the outdoors and for the arts, two passions that play a major role in my life. My mother didn't garden or play golf or tennis. In fact, she didn't even drive and so she walked a lot, every day. Sometimes when I'd had a doctor's appointment and was late for school, she'd walk there with me to keep me company. And because she couldn't chauffeur me around, she encouraged me to walk or to ride my bike or to take public transportation. I learned to be very independent.

We didn't have much of a garden but my father lovingly tended the half-dozen rosebushes that lined the short walk to our front porch. With those roses, he planted the seed of my lifelong love of flowers. I think of my dad often when I work in my garden.

My mother's father had a small upholstery shop and it was there that my mother developed her love for texture and weave. She passed it on to me. When I was a child, she shlepped me with her to tiny fabric shops and large warehouses crammed with bolts of color fabric. From my mother, I learned the difference between jacquard and flame stitching, between moiré and pique, and why a certain fabric would or wouldn't work for a given project.

Mom would collect snips and samples—there was always a chair that needed to be covered or a pillow to be made. But my mother, for all her endearing qualities, was incredibly and maddeningly indecisive. We lived with swatches of fabric thrown over the sofa or chairs, samples that were never used. It might have been years before a piece got reupholstered but I certainly didn't care—my dolls had some pretty fancy clothing. Those early years gave me an appreciation of fine textiles. They explain why one of my favorite outings is to the wholesale fabric district where I can touch the silks and tapestries and dream up new projects for my own home.

Music is another passion of mine that came from my parents. In our house, the radio played incessantly. One of my earliest memories is of sitting in front of the console radio in our living room, enraptured by the great tenor voice of Mario Lanza, whom I imitated dramatically, driving my family nuts. Most of the time, we tuned to classical music. On Saturday afternoons, Mom listened to opera. On Sunday mornings, the Jewish hour was as ubiquitous as the breakfast bagels and lox. I was introduced to a large repertoire of Jewish folk music. Although neither of my parents played an instrument, they recognized my talent and encouraged me through twelve years of piano lessons. Neither Mom nor Dad had a particularly lyrical voice but they both loved to sing. During Sunday drives, Dad would croon Irish melodies and belt out show tunes or his favorite, his college drinking song. The dinner dishes were ritually done each evening with Mom washing and me drying, the both of us warbling "La donna è mobile" or "Oifn Pripetshik," a beloved Yiddish lullaby. My lifelong love of music was cemented in those evenings. The legacy of those memories, in the interests they fostered, is far more precious than the sterling serving pieces or wing chair that now grace my home.

These are the kind of memories that define the nature of our legacy, that characterize the origin of our individual interests. As Jill recalls, "My mother had a wonderful eye for beauty. She observed nature keenly—the color of this plant or that flower. My brother also has this gift of observation. He takes beautiful photographs. He takes ordinary things and makes them look extraordinary."

So evident was Jill's mother's love of the beauty in nature that her ten-year-old grandchild, who shared a close relationship with her grandmother, remarked after her death, "when people are in heaven, they have jobs and Grandma must be in charge of beauty. Whenever we walk in the park and see a pond with sun glistening, that's Grandma's work."

Indeed, it seems that the appreciation of beauty has been bequeathed to future generations in Jill's family.

Love of Family and Home

Donna's parents, so vibrant and fun loving, left their five daughters a legacy of love of family and home life that has framed Donna's entire adult life. Her midlife divorce was a bitter disappointment but her capacity for joie de vivre has enabled her to fill her home with joy, with or without a husband.

"My father was very much in love with my mother. He was about twelve years older than she was. He told us how he used to wait for her to come back from other dates, because he was dating her sister," says this fifty-five-year-old actress, flashing a bright smile.

Donna recalls her parents' harmonious domesticity. "When they got married, they had a house. Even before they moved in, it was all set up, very organized, they had the linens all put away. My father was very much into the home. My mother was a typical mother hen. She never worked but she loved to cook, to have company, and everyone liked to talk to her. Once she struck up a conversation with a woman on a bus in Italy and, the next thing we knew, the woman and her daughter were here visiting us."

Smiling at her recollections, Donna continues, "Every time I cook chicken, I think of my mother because when I was young, she'd put me up on a stool so I could play in the junk drawer, next to the double sink, when she was cleaning the chickens. She'd say to me as she worked, 'See, this is the little heart.' "

Donna laughs. "I couldn't understand how she could do that. She was a good cook—she cooked by instinct. I'm the only one [of the siblings] who makes Thanksgiving stuffing like hers. Maybe because she used to paint, like I do, we could relate. I remember I was talking to her on the phone and we were both looking at the clouds and she said that they looked like cauliflower. She always noticed nature. She had a terrific eye. She'd notice things that no one else would."

Donna's home is filled with plants and the multitude of oil paintings that she has been creating for more than a decade. A friend drops by and Donna issues a dinner invitation. He comments to me about her wonderful cooking. The phone rings incessantly. It is apparent that she is at the hub of a social life shared with a roster of close friends. Of her artistic soul, Donna says she is much like her parents in the way she looks at other people: "I don't notice clothes, I notice something about the face."

Donna sees her artistic nature as her parents' bequest. She continues to embrace their passion for life, relishing any opportunity to share it with friends and family. This is the legacy that Donna's parents left her, and in her home, the legacy endures.

Genetic Link

At no time does our likeness to our parents become more obvious than after they are gone, as we ourselves begin to age. What once was a slight familial similarity now becomes an uncanny resemblance. We can argue whether or not our wrinkles and gray hair add character, but there is no disputing that they breed a certain familiar likeness. With the loss of our parents, we begin to notice how much we resemble Mom or Dad or the way that our voice, even more than the words we speak, has come to sound like theirs.

For more than a year after my mother died, each time I glanced in the mirror I saw her face staring back at me. Since there had never been much of a physical resemblance, it came as a bit of a shock. The face in the mirror looked old and tired, the droopy cheeks formed deep parentheses around my smile. I wanted my own face back. The resemblance to my mother was somewhat disconcerting. It's a sentiment I heard other midlife orphans describe.

Five years have passed and I am myself again. Although the signs of aging, quite frankly, are less than thrilling, I take solace in the fact that my hair, like that of my folks, is slow to turn gray. Photos of my parents in their late sixties show hair only slightly peppered with gray. Inspired by one of those photographs (and a color mishap), I decided to let the blonde highlighting I'd had for more than thirty years grow out. It was fun to discover that my natural color, a dirty blonde the last time I'd seen it, had become a deep chestnut with a hint of red and only a very few gray hairs. Trivial perhaps, but it's a link to my parents that makes me feel good.

We used to joke in our family that we were of hardy stock. I believed that until the day my father's Alzheimer's was diagnosed. But as I watched the progression of the disease, I fought a growing fear that this disease was in my future. It didn't help when my kids teased me about my failing memory.

For better or for worse, our parents' health and their deaths afford us some kind of fitness meter, a prompt to evaluate our own health. I remember how angry I was the day my mother's brain tumor was diagnosed, when my sister jokingly said to me, "Well, our genetic makeup's not looking so good."

For the first time in my life, I became overly concerned about my own health. I questioned a sudden headache, a pain in my side, a crick in my neck. I probably saw my doctor more in those first two years after my parents died than ever before. But in time, after enough tests, I could acknowledge that, indeed, I am of hardy stock. Like my parents who were rarely sick until their final illnesses, I am healthy. My father was eighty when he died from the accident—his brain was addled by Alzheimer's but he had no physical problems. My parents lived, until their deaths, free from disabling physical ailments. That neither died painlessly saddens me terribly. But finally, I am able to look back and focus on their long, healthy lives instead of the illnesses that killed them. With our hardy stock and my healthy lifestyle, I am optimistic that I will be around for a long time.

Paula, attractive and vivacious at fifty-nine, says, "I look in the mirror and although I never looked like my mother before, now I feel like I do. I was the last one to wear glasses in my family. I never felt old 'til now. My mother used to sit in this same wing-back chair and when I sit here, I look just like her. I sometimes think she's somehow in here with me."

Eyeing our children, we see a glint of the past generation, of parents who are now gone. When I had to address Andy at his Bar Mitzvah, I said what was truly in my heart: "You have said many times that you are sorry Mom-mom isn't here. But I can tell you that she is very much here, for I see her in your smile and in the compassion that you show for others."

It was so true. Why did I never see that while she was alive? Andy's physical likeness to his father's side was so great that I never noticed this other familial link. Yet, his smile, his self-deprecating humor and compassion are my mother's. Nor did I recognize that my older son Dan's quiet dogged ability to focus is my father's, although I'd figured that his math and engineering ability were in part inherited from him. Of course, I know that some of what my children have is of their father, some of me. But now when I look at my sons, for some inexplicable reason, I see in each both my mother and my father as much as I recognize their father and myself.

But what happens when there is no genetic link? If we are adopted or we have adopted children, there is an added dimension of loss that the rest of us don't experience when our last parent dies. For instance, Elaine was sixteen when her mother died. It was a devastating loss, made all the more so when, at nineteen, Elaine first learned of her adoption. Elaine remarks that her mother remains fixed in her memory as the young woman she was at her death. Elaine knew her only as a mother and what she knew was from her experience as a teenager. It was too early for her to experience her mother as a woman, especially since her mother had chosen not to share the fact that she'd adopted Elaine. As Hope Edelman wrote in *Motherless Daughters,* "a daughter knows about her mother only as much as both of them want her to learn."[38]

When Elaine's father died just a few years ago, friends wondered whether Elaine would finally seek out her birth mother. Elaine resents the idea. She feels that she had wonderful parents and sees no reason to seek out the mother who gave her up for adoption. She imagines that her birth mother was quite young and did what she thought was best, but she has no interest in finding her. Learning of her adoption was a great shock to Elaine. At the time, her father, in a conciliatory gesture, offered to help her if she wanted to search for her birth mother. Although Elaine has, at times, wished for more information regarding medical history, her curiosity is not pressing enough to make her look for her natural mother. For Elaine, the legacy of love, support, and nurturing is with her, so the lack of a genetic link to her parents does not disturb her. Elaine knows that in her own child, although she bears no resemblance to her grandparents, is invested a legacy of love and values that Elaine got from her own parents.

For Donna, however, the lack of blood ties from her family to her adopted son is something that she wrestles with. Donna and her ex-husband adopted their son, Alberto, at infancy. Since her mother's death, as she has increasingly noticed the family resemblance in herself, Donna is more bothered by the lack of familial links to her son, even though his remarkable resemblance to her ex-husband belies his adoption. Donna finds that her son's questioning about family traits is comforting. "When Alberto asked me if my father was bald and I told him no, he said, 'Oh good, 'cause I don't want to be bald.' Even though he knows he's adopted, he still asks questions like that."

At the beginning of our interview, I mention to Donna that my son's smile, so much like my mother's, gives me great comfort. She answers, longingly, "I envy you because that's something I'll never have. Once when Alberto was about five, he cut his finger and I held it and sucked on it. I remember thinking, 'He doesn't have any of me in him but now I have him in me.' Sometimes it bothers me because I realize there's no little piece of me to leave. My older sister said that it doesn't really matter that he's not my natural child, that kids are kids but . . . ," her voice trails off.

"But I'll tell you," she adds regaining her delightful sense of humor, "if he wants to find his biological mother, that's fine. Because then I'd try to find the biological father, 'cause this is one great-looking kid."

For Donna, whose love for her son is wholehearted, there remains a tiny, unquiet spot deep inside that regrets that neither her parents' genes nor her own will be carried to the next generation through her child.

Legacy of Traditions

"When I was growing up we had lots of these traditions, especially for Christmas. Like on Christmas morning, we always had this sausage and egg casserole. I still make it for Christmas breakfast. It's something that my boys look forward to, even though they're now in their twenties. In fact, about six years ago we were going out of town to meet family that was flying in and I said something about having the casserole a few days before Christmas instead. My son was like, 'Gosh, Mom, it won't be Christmas without it.' So I think maybe someday he'll say to his wife, 'You know, we have to have this sausage and egg casserole for Christmas morning.' It's that type of thing that got passed down from my parents. And we always go to church on Christmas Eve together like we did at my house as I was growing up. We decorate the tree together also. When I was in middle school, my parents started giving each child an ornament every year so I've done that with my kids."

The words tumble out as Randi happily recalls these holiday memories. She is talking about the legacy of holiday tradition that her parents established for her and that she has lovingly carried out with her own family. Bess also recalls special times in a home where family time was a luxury. With her parents working totally opposite shifts, there was only one day a week for the family to be together. But birthdays were always set aside for celebration, no matter what.

"Birthdays you always got your special dinner," Bess recalls. "My grandmother cooked and we always sat down at the table together."

For Jay, at no time does his parents' legacy exert more influence than on holidays and birthdays. That's when the family "has to" be together, according to Jay. "It's about making that special effort to be there, whether it's Christmas, or spring break, or on a birthday. It's just the importance of, you know, just being there with family. You just have to try and get together with family."

For Jay, just as it is for Randi, Christmas is "a big deal." He explains that since his parents' deaths, he and his siblings make a special effort to continue to serve some of the ethnic food they grew up with, the legacy of their Ukrainian grandparents. On holidays, the family dines on cabbage rolls and pirogies although things aren't quite the same as when his parents were alive. Jay chuckles as he explains that his English wife can't be bothered preparing these ethnic specialties. And so she buys the family favorites at a local shop, a place they discovered that makes up great cabbage rolls, almost as good as the ones Jay's grandmother used to make.

Jay continues, "This past year, my daughter took a real interest in my mother's china because it had been packed away for her. She got it all out the day before Mother's Day and asked if we could use Grandma's china. So we got it all out, washed it all up, and we used that for Mother's Day—traditions like that are very important. It really kind of made me feel great that, you know, here's our dining room set up with Grandma's china. It was like being back home again. We talked a lot about why things like that were important and what memories the china brought back."

"Easter was the holiday that I always remember," begins Sheila. "My mother always made these little bunny footprints with flowers from the front door to our Easter baskets. It was really cute. So I always did the same thing for my kids. And then, I guess about two years ago, I quit doing it because I figured these kids are too big for this. And my sons were probably freshmen in college at that point. They were home for Easter vacation and had gone out with their buddies. The next morning I got up and there were bunny prints from the door to the Easter basket. The kids did it for me; it was just such a sweet thing.

"I guess, more than anything since they [her parents] have been gone, I've just realized that these traditions and values, they're the only thing you've got left when it's all over. And you've got to pass those things on to your family."

The Legacy of Parenting

Jill is talking about some of the things that her parents did that she continues to do with her children today: "When my son was little, I had an incredible repertoire of kids' songs and ditties that I got from my parents. Some were long and complicated yet I remembered every word. Although I hadn't practiced or thought about them for thirty or forty years, when my son was born they just came back to me. I found that fascinating. And you find yourself saying things that your parents said, like, 'Good night, don't let the bedbugs bite.' "

No matter how our parenting style differs from our parents', there is no denying that some of our style comes from them. Our parents probably didn't give us "time out"—that was a concept of the seventies. But the way they disciplined probably influences how we discipline our children. If our parents were democratic, then it is likely that informal family meetings are part of our routine. If our parents were autocratic and ruled by fear, it shouldn't come as a surprise that we discipline in much the same way. Whether it is in the nursery rhymes we read to our children, the songs we sing, or the foods we feed them, we model ourselves after what we knew best, the parents who raised us.

For George, his parents' belief that "education is everything" is the driving force behind the decision to send his children to private school that he and his wife can barely afford.

"They knew that education is the ticket to a more secure future. My mother's mother was a teacher and her aunt was a principal. You couldn't have too much education; the more you got, the better you were going to be," recalls George.

Of the way he and his wife parent, George explains, "We gush over our children. My parents didn't do that. They were much more guarded in their praise. My mother would come at it from the other way, asking what I was doing and what I'm singing these days. My father was fairly straightforward but they didn't show a lot of the effusiveness that we do."

George and his wife may praise their children with more enthusiasm than his parents did but George learned the value of praise from his parents. Even though George regards the way that he and his wife parent as so different from their own parents, it becomes evident as we speak that the style may be different but the substance is the same. In their own way, George's parents were as involved in his life as he is with his children. His parents taught him life lessons that George's children take for granted.

George continues, "I want to be with my children, I mean I really want to be with them. I like experiencing what they experience. My parents used to say 'Okay, go outside and play.' You know, that was what we did, we just went outside and played. Children were seen and not heard. It's just very different with us."

But the South in the nineteen fifties, where George grew up, wasn't quite the same as the suburban neighborhood that is home to George's children. Until he finished junior high school, George had to use a separate entrance to the local movie theater from the one his white friends used. He remembers "colored water fountains" and separate bathrooms and riding in the back of the bus.

"I'm glad that my parents taught us what they did, that everybody was the same. They taught us that some people were more stupid than others, and the people who were stupid were the ones who were discriminatory and they weren't bad, just ignorant. So, they made a distinction between people being bad as opposed to being stupid. They said there are ignorant people of all colors. My parents just said that everybody's entitled to an opinion but what you do is up to you."

In the racially mixed neighborhood in which they lived, his

parents refused to foster any idea that George and his brother were different. Perhaps that's why they encouraged their boys to "go out and play." They may have known that the best way for their sons to learn about the world was to go out and conquer it.

The Legacy of Grandchildren

"After his last grandparent died, my thirteen-year-old actually listened when I started talking about reaching out to some of my cousins. He really thinks that would be fun. So I ordered a family tree thing, just to put it down, some of the connections and who the cousins are."

Sheila is talking about her child's reaction to the loss of his grandparents. She found, to her astonishment, that her son developed an active interest in the family when her last parent died. Suddenly, distant cousins and relatives became important. He began to ask lots of questions, many that she couldn't answer.

If we allow our children to articulate that loss, we may be surprised by what we learn. For our children, grandparents represent history and continuity. They are filled with tales of "the olden days." Theirs is a wisdom that is more respected than our own—it's fun to interview grandparents for a school project. And grandparents are about love and being spoiled, not about discipline.

Marge describes her daughter's relationship with her grandmother: "My daughter had a nice relationship with my mother. She'd go over her grandmother's for lunch and sleep over at her house. They'd play cards together. My mother taught her the few cooking skills that she has; I certainly didn't. But she didn't have the same warmth with her grandson, I'm not sure why."

"My mother had a way of bringing that soft side out of my

daughter which I couldn't. My daughter was very close to my mother because her grandmother always saw the sweet side of her." Cass has always been grateful for the relationship between her mother and her daughter, who was a very difficult adolescent. She feels that her mother was able to nurture her granddaughter at a time when she needed it and wouldn't accept it from anyone else.

"When I called to tell them [her sons] that Nana had died, Eric started to cry because he said he was sad that I didn't have any parents anymore. That made me feel good, like I'm really important to him. So I told my other son what his brother said and I admitted that not having any parents made me feel kind of sad. He says to me, 'Yeah, but you're old enough. You can take care of yourself.' He wasn't going to feel bad, no matter what. Two different kids, totally different reactions." Shelley laughs at the recollection.

It's not unusual for grandchildren to experience the loss of grandparents as the loss of their parent's parents—kids don't like to see their parents unhappy. Maybe it's easier than feeling the reality of death. Or perhaps it's really about the individual way that we mourn. Or simply about the relationship between the individual grandchild and his grandparents. Some of it has to do with the age that our children are when their grandparents die.

However our children feel about the loss of their grandparents, it's up to us, their parents, to foster the relationship, if only in memory. As Sheila says, "After your parents die, I guess you realize that life is so fleeting, that it becomes important to leave a legacy to your own children. I feel bad for people who don't have children. It helped me when my parents died to know that I had four children to leave the legacy of what my mother and father had left me."

Journal Entry, November 14, 1992

We are sitting at the dinner table, my sons and I. It is a few days after the doctor diagnosed my mother's brain tumor. They will need to perform a biopsy. We don't have much information yet but it doesn't look good.

Andy, eleven, raises his fork to his neck, dripping spaghetti sauce on his white T-shirt.

"Is Mom-mom going to . . . ?" he asks, making a slicing motion across his neck.

His older brother slugs him in the side.

"Is she going to . . . what?" Dan challenges.

Andy is quiet.

"Are you asking if she's going to die?" I question.

He nods.

"Why don't you just say it?" taunts Dan.

"I don't like the word," Andy says softly.

"Me neither," I agree.

Nobody speaks for a moment.

"Are you afraid, Mom?" Dan asks.

"What do you mean?"

"I mean, you know, are you afraid to be alone, without a mom and dad?"

I sigh.

"Well, here I am a grown-up with kids of my own and it's impossible for me to imagine not having any parents. I can't fathom it. So I guess in a way, I am afraid."

"But you won't be alone, Mom. You'll still have us," the boys chime in simultaneously, as if rehearsed.

Thank you, God, for these children.

CHANGING RELATIONSHIPS

$\mathcal{F}$ or most of the adult orphans I interviewed, life after parents takes on a decidedly different feel. While our daily lives and routine may not be altered, we experience, at a gut level, subtle changes in our relationships with siblings, children, spouse, friends—and ourselves. Most of the time, the change is not so much in the way we relate or interact, rather, the change occurs within oneself. The death of the last parent, with its sweeping impact, signals the end of an era. With this new awareness of our mortality, relationships take on a new importance.

Without parents, the family dynamic inevitably shifts. The adult children's relationships with each other may falter without the glue that parents provided. On the other hand, years of parental influence may serve to hold the family together. Siblings who are close generally remain that way, bound together even more by their collective memories and shared history. Siblings who have enjoyed the love and support of parents may now provide similar support for each other. But what of siblings whose relationship has not been altogether positive? There is no way to predict what will happen to these relationships. Some make a conscious decision to try to become closer. Others may try but a history of peevish interactions prevails. As we have seen, the inheritance can serve as the catalyst to tear apart faltering sibling relationships.

In the interviews I conducted, most of the sibling relationships pretty much remained the same as they were before parents' deaths. What did change was the desire to try to mend relationships.

Changes in Family Relationships

One of my favorite family photos shows three strikingly attractive women with bouffant pageboys, the two dark-haired ones flanking the champagne blonde. Svelte in floor-length beaded evening gowns, they beam megawatt smiles and stand with arms entwined, slightly turned to one side, posed like a celebrity trio. They are my mother and her two sisters, so closely resembling each other with their handsome looks, their distinctive brand of humor, and their flair for fashion that they were dubbed "the Gabor sisters." The photo was taken thirty years ago, at my sister's wedding. Today only Mitzi, the youngest of the sisters, is living.

Months go by that I don't see my aunt, who resides at the seashore less than an hour away, but rarely does more than a week pass that we don't speak on the phone. She is the closest living reminder of Mom. The bond and affection between Mitzi, my mother, and their sister Jesse, who died in 1985, defined our frequent family gatherings. Together, the sisters provided memorable meals and a terrific shared sense of humor that kept everyone entertained. In our family, the men remained in the background, no match for the sisters, who blossomed in each other's presence. Through years and layers of family tragedies, their relationship endured and strengthened as they supported and comforted one another.

After my mother died, it seemed perfectly natural for me to turn to her younger sibling to fill the need I had for a mother figure. We have always had a close relationship. My memories include summer visits to her house, where she doted on me, always lavishing me with hugs and kisses. As similar as she was to my mother, the nine years between them was enough to allow me to relate to my aunt differently. To me, she was a more fun version of my mother, familiar but without all the angst—precisely what an aunt should be. When I got older, we curled up on the bed to chitchat, just as I had always seen her do with her sisters. Like my mother, she is a "hugger." We still sprawl and she continues to be as affectionate as ever but our relationship has changed. Long-distance calls . . . nobody cares about cost anymore. Our weekly phone calls fill a need for me but it is no longer a need for a mother figure. Instead, I call her because she is more than an aunt to me, she has become a friend. Perhaps because she was younger than my mother, she is more able to talk about feelings. Through her, I have come to understand better who my mother was.

Mitzi takes her role as my aunt earnestly—she and my uncle show the concern for my sons that my parents did. They wouldn't have missed Dan's high school graduation for anything. Andy refers to them as his "surrogate grandparents." My aunt and uncle cannot replace my parents but they brighten the dark space left by their absence. They are the last of that generation in our family, so our time together becomes more precious with each year.

In the past twelve years, my losses have been great—in addition to my parents, my mother's other sister and her husband and two of their sons died. I also mourned a family for whom I had very warm feelings, lost to the ravages of divorce. With my family of origin now so diminished, I cling to the tiny surviving core. We are bonded by memories of decades of family gatherings and holidays spent together. And we are all too aware of the fragility of relationships and how temporal life is. As a result, we grasp at every opportunity to celebrate together.

Once parents are gone, we may find ourselves tweaking our relationships with aunts, uncles, and cousins. Sometimes we seek out relatives, sometimes we reject them, or we may just drift apart. Much depends on our history and whether our parents encouraged and reinforced those relationships. And obviously, some of the outcome depends upon our individual needs. Many of us are caught off guard by this need to connect once our last parent dies.

Allie remained close to her mother's sister when she found herself orphaned after her mother died several years ago. But Allie longed for more family contact. She began to actively go out to create new networks with her cousins and her cousins' children. She explains, "I'm weaving new relationships with them and I'm even taking a course in family relationships and figuring out how to make our family work better. In fact, I'm dedicating this year to it, investing in something that is going to go somewhere." Allie is thrilled that her West Coast cousins' daughter, now living in Washington, D.C., will be spending the Thanksgiving holiday with her this year. The threads she is weaving are beginning to form new family tapestries.

Mark continues to be the pivotal figure in a family that was at one time very close-knit. Growing up in New Jersey, Mark's family spent almost every weekend with his mother's sisters and brother, who lived in neighboring towns. But years and geography put distance between the relatives. After Mark's father died, Mark was acutely aware of the waning family and he made a concerted effort to be more in touch with them. Mark smiles as he offers, "It's nice to reestablish, especially with my uncle. And it's funny how we reestablished with my mother's youngest sister's daughter. I even went to her wedding in New Zealand last year— the only relative who went."

While such heartwarming efforts enrich our lives, the outcome is sometimes something more than we bargained for. Reaching out to extended family can result in additional responsibility, as it has for Mark. His cousin, with whom he now shares a warm friendship, urges Mark from her home on the other side of the world to look after her parents and visit them frequently. The four- to five-hour drive to their home is taxing for Mark, who works long hours, travels often for business, and hates driving.

He adds, "My aunt's got no kids around and she has this immobile husband. She wants me to find a place here for her—they want to move down here. I'm like, 'Oh, my God, then what?' I feel worse about these folks than I ever felt about my parents because we used to be very close and they're almost pleading for me to do something. It's like I'll fix it for them. I won't but they think I will."

Does Mark really feel guiltier about his caretaking for his aunt and uncle than he did about his own parents, as he says? No, of course not. But he understands that his obligation to his parents required no decision on his part—it went without saying that he would take care of them. It is not Mark's responsibility to care for his relatives, yet his compassion and love of family give him no choice. Mark is coming to terms with his values, and it is obvious that, where family is concerned, he is a very humane, caring man.

Not everyone can be like Mark. Often, in our initial grief over the loss of the last parent, we don't have much energy for relationships. If the family doesn't make an effort to reach out to us, we are likely to let the relationship go. Later, when we are emotionally and physically restored, we may decide to reinvent the family, as Heidi has done. A couple of years after her last parent's death, a longing for more attachment stirred in Heidi. It became important that her daughter's childhood should be more like her own, shared with cousins and extended family. The desire for that connection was worth the effort of reaching out to family whom she felt had abandoned her somewhat after her last parent's death.

Heidi comments, "My father's side didn't call much after he died. They just sort of drifted away. I started communicating with them a few years ago. I missed having an extended family and Sarah [her seven-year-old daughter] has some cousins there so it's nice for her."

Like Heidi's desire for her daughter to know her cousins, George also wants his children to get to know their family better. He says, "It's terrible, I called my brother the other day and said that I wanted to go down and see him because 'my kids won't even know who you are if we don't visit more.' " George's niece is only a month older than his son and George feels badly that the cousins have spent so little time together. Since his last parent died, George refers to his life on the eastern seaboard as "out of control, crazed, like a battery on fast forward." He is much more conscious of time passing and would like to spend more time with family.

Adult orphans like Heidi, Mark, and George have made a point to reach out to family after the death of their parents. However, as midlife orphans move through the process of evaluating our lives, many decide that it's time to cast out certain family members or friends. Those who have disappointed us may not make the cut. In the period after the last parent's death, we pare down who and what we perceive as truly worthy of our emotional investment. We begin to carve out new relationships and redefine "family."

As Portia matured, she realized that her parents had lived their lives with "obligations," as she defined their need to keep up relationships that were less than satisfying. Portia didn't share her parents' sense of duty for duty's sake and after her father's death, she severed certain family relationships. Even though she is an only child and a single mother, she has been willing to reduce the extent of family contact. Portia explains, "I cut those obligations so my family group includes just those people I've chosen. In some ways, I live without strings, although it would be nice to have more of those ties. You know, when I met Barry's [her significant other] mother last year on vacation, I stayed with her when she lagged behind, when he had no patience. I was happy to spend time with her—not just because it was his mother. I told him that she's a neat lady." Portia is brutally honest when she acknowledges that her behavior was totally self-serving, "a no-strings relationship."

In contrast to those who feel that the death of the last parent offers an opportunity to end unsatisfying relationships, some mid-life orphans like Nanci prefer to become peacemakers, patching up old family feuds. When Nanci's father died twenty years earlier, her mother argued with some of the relatives and, as a result, Nanci and her sister were estranged from that side of the family. Her son's approaching Bar Mitzvah heightened Nanci's sense of loss, as life events tend to do. She decided to invite aunts, uncles, and cousins that she hadn't seen in many years, to celebrate this joyous event with her family. To her bemusement, not only did they gladly accept her invitation, somehow, they misread the date and descended on her a week early.

One particular aspect of the Bar Mitzvah triggered a deep emotional response for Nanci. A tradition in their synagogue passes the Torah (the sacred scroll) from one generation to another. With both parents and in-laws deceased, there were no grandparents to participate in this ritual. Nanci asked her mother's brother to assume the role of the "older" generation.

Nanci recalls, "It felt like such an empty hole with no grandparents there. When you look around at these family funerals, you start to realize how important your family is. I've lived away from most of my family for about fifteen years. So when I would go to these funerals, I got connected more with the uncles and the cousins and I kind of started to realize how important they are. Now that I don't have parents in my hometown area, I have to really make an effort now to be sure I keep in contact with the rest of the family."

Nanci believes these relationships with extended family enhance the fabric of her life and are worth the effort. Her sister, Shelley, however, does not share her feelings. Because Shelley and Nanci were caretakers for their emotionally difficult, widowed mother for much of their adolescence, Shelley relishes the freedom that she has now. She fears that involvement with her relatives will eventually thrust her into a caretaking role. She is not anxious to find herself in that position again, especially for family with whom she does not feel particularly close.

On those occasions when someone in the family reveals a side that is distasteful (as often happens with issues revolving around an inheritance), many feel it is grounds for a permanent whiteout. For example, Portia had no qualms about renouncing her relationship with a cousin whose chutzpah floored her. Surmising that Portia received a small inheritance when her last parent died, this cousin called to borrow money so that his son could buy a house. Portia was sickened by the fact that he made this appeal while she was sitting Shiva (the week-long mourning period that Jews observe) for her father. As a result of that incident, Portia says, "I won't have anything to do with him. I'm civil when I see him but that's all."

Portia made a decision that felt right for her. In doing so, she has not rejected her parents' values. Instead, like other midlife orphans who wrestle with relationship changes after the last parent's death, Portia has integrated her parents' values into her own. She holds a firm belief in family, much as her parents did, but Portia wants her relationships to be more significant. To her, those that are less meaningful are expendable. Reconstructing the family circle can cause great pain or reap a joyous return. But as many midlife orphans discover, it is far easier to deal with the aunts, uncles, and cousins from whom we are somewhat removed than it is to deal with a brother or sister with whom we shared a bedroom in the most formative period of our life.

My Brother's Keeper: The Sibling Relationship

"I think my sister is happier with herself now. She probably thought Mom favored me. I think Mom treated us equally, considering that we were different and that Mom and I just instinctively got along better. We were on the same wavelength and she and my sister weren't. So now that whole barrier is gone." Margot, a forty-seven-year-old photographer, is reflecting on her previously testy relationship with her older sister. Their mother, you may recall from a previous chapter, was widowed when the girls were young.

As adults living on separate coasts, the sisters did not have to confront their past, which was speckled with rivalry, until their mother became terminally ill. At that point, the relational patterns of the past began to emerge. Margot, the doting daughter who also lived near her mother, carried the burden of responsibility for her care. Delia, her older sister, had always resented her younger sister, whose talents she felt she could never match. When Delia flew in from her home on the West Coast, she appeared to be somewhat detached from the situation and her attitude infuriated Margot. Delia comments that she has never been very expressive with sad emotions. She contends that she was not uncaring, as her sister perceived her. Instead, she realized how close to death their mother was and was relieved that she wasn't going to suffer.

Delia explains, "I knew she was going to die. I figured it was a good thing because she wasn't ever going to get back to where she was. Lots of people had the same reaction as my sister. They were annoyed with me because I didn't seem so devastated."

Delia reflects on the tension with her sister, "One of the things my mother did was to tell me I had to be better than my little sister to set an example. Margot was the athletic one. I was the fat, dumpy one with artistic interests. For me to try to be better than her was a futile exercise. Margot had a similar onus placed on her but of course we didn't know that 'til after Mom died. So there was a built-in competition for nearly fifty years. After Mom died and we started talking it out, we changed things. Lots of what we had heard was filtered through our mother. It's been an unexpected but positive consequence of her death. And since Margot has remarried, we've gotten even closer."

Delia and Margot continue to reshape their relationship. They may never be best friends but they are now sisters who can speak openly to each other, working to bury the competitive rivalry that plagued their relationship for too many years.

Left without parents to define the relationship for them, siblings may give voice to their own feelings about its nature. Mom and Dad may have wanted to believe that their children got along fine. Perhaps they wanted to believe that their parenting was responsible for tight sibling relationships. They may have urged the siblings to get along and to overlook dissension, "for the sake of the family." To please parents, many children keep up the front that all is well. Much of this depends upon the individual's temperament and own needs. Some of it is circumstantial. For example, Lani feels that her relationship with many of her eight siblings is superficial and not particularly satisfying emotionally. Her older brother Seth perceives their relationships quite differently.

Seth comments, "My parents encouraged us to be loyal to each other. We were always to be there. If there was a problem with one of us growing up in the neighborhood with somebody else, we all stuck together. We all dealt with it, you know, kind of as a group and so when there are joyous things that happen we all come together. When there are sad things, we come together."

The disparity between Seth's and Lani's perceptions of the sibling relationship in their family probably stems from family history that continues to haunt them. You may recall that, as a teen, Lani was removed from the family home and placed with an older sibling and her husband and children when their parents' alcoholism became intolerable. Lani resented her siblings' intervention and regrets her refusal to stand up to them. Seth, on the other hand, feels that he and his siblings did what was best for their sister. Of all the children, Lani feels that she was closest to their mother. Her disappointment in her siblings is related to expectations that she feels they didn't meet for her when she was growing up and after their last parent's death.

In addition, the age gap between Seth and the older siblings and Lani and her younger brother almost made it seem like they were two distinct families. While Seth and most of his siblings lived in the house together, they had moved out by the time Lani and their youngest brother were growing up. Consequently, Lani's experience in the family was markedly different from Seth's.

While some siblings like Delia and Margot have been able to

successfully alter their relationship after the last parent's death, many adults feel that they are incapable of changing the sibling relationship, either because of their own inadequacies or their siblings' shortcomings. Often, a lifetime of poor communication is a pattern that seems impossible to change. However, rather than keep the status quo or end the relationship, some siblings find themselves developing a degree of tolerance or acceptance that wasn't there previously, in order to hold the family together. There is a desire to spend more time together, to be a family, even if the dynamics of the relationship are difficult to change.

As Cass says, "I've always had a distant relationship with my younger sister, who's ten years younger. My other sister and I always believed that our parents thought that our younger sister was the perfect one. She lives in the South and wasn't really around when my parents were sick so we had some resentment about that. But now we all consciously try to keep in touch. Before, we always saw each other but only at Christmas. But now, we'll congregate more. Our younger sister's daughter is going to college near here so my sister will visit. I'm just crazy about my niece but, 'til now, I've only seen her a once a year."

Lynda is learning to accept and enjoy a brother with whom she has had a relatively superficial adult relationship. Before their mother died, she and her brother rarely spent time together. Generally, phone calls were limited to exchanging information. Lynda feels that their mother favored her son even though, for most of her adult life (until her mother stopped speaking to her), Lynda had more responsibility for her mother than her brother did. But largely as a result of their experience cleaning out their mother's apartment after her death, when they were able to spend long hours together laughing and sharing memories, Lynda has consciously altered the relationship, putting past resentments behind her. She and her brother work harder at their relationship. They visit back and forth more, and Lynda joins her brother and his wife for dinner or an evening of theater. They even overlapped a vacation in the West together.

Says Lynda, "I do make more of an effort to be closer to my brother now. I'll call more often. I accept that he's not going to talk about certain things. In that way, he's a lot like my mother. He seems easygoing but he has a temper and he can be passive-aggressive when he wants to be. But we spent serious bonding time together cleaning out my mother's apartment and it was fun. We were reminiscing and laughing."

Without parents, even siblings who have little in common find themselves drawn to each other, connected by a shared past. In some cases, like that of Marcia and her brother, the past was painful. Although Marcia and her brother do not talk much about it, they share the knowledge that their upbringing was neither normal nor healthy. When they were just young children, their father died and their mother separated the children, farming them out to distant relatives for long periods of time as she struggled to pull her life together. For the most part, Marcia and her older brother did not grow up together. Today, they live in worlds that are vastly disparate. Marcia is an educator and is politically active on the local level. Her brother had a limited education, got a job, and married very young. The siblings kept in touch sporadically through the years but their relationship could hardly be characterized as close. While her brother basically had no relationship with their mother, Marcia ended up as her primary caretaker for the last twenty years until her death. Nonetheless, Marcia appreciated the fact that her brother respected her efforts in their mother's declining years. Since their mother's death, Marcia and her brother chat more often. Marcia has become more involved with her brother's family and enjoys infrequent visits with his children.

Marcia explains, "My brother hasn't been a support system for me but he's been very decent. He's never criticized anything I've done. And when it came to splitting up my mother's things, he said to 'keep what's left, you've done all the work.' I told him at the funeral that I wasn't dealing with the furniture or clothing, that I was giving it all to the woman who took care of our mother, and he said, 'Whatever you want to do.' I wanted her to have it because she was there for my mother."

When the relationship has been good, siblings are a tremendous source of support to each other as they enter the caretaking years for their parents. Generally, those siblings continue to be supportive after the last parent's death. Shelley describes how she and her older sister worked together during their mother's final illness. "I think there was at least a phone call every day. For a year and a half, we just did it [cared for their mother]. I don't think she felt more burdened than I felt. We could just share our feelings about it and that was great. It helped me feel more connected to my sister."

In a joint interview, Shelley and her sister agreed that despite the five years' difference between them, they have always been close, allied in their mutual defense of their widowed mother's emotional instability. Nanci, as the older sister, provided the nurturing for Shelley that their mother could not. She willingly took Shelley along to ball games and activities with her friends. Today the sisters remain connected by their shared history and their determination to keep their relationship intact.

An Only Child Reaches Out

For an only child, the loss of the last parent can be particularly lonely. That is why Bess, who is divorced and has no children, finds herself increasingly more attached to her stepsiblings—her father's children from an earlier marriage. It wasn't until she was in high school that Bess learned of their existence—their mother had taken the children from her husband and he never saw them until they sought him out years later. Bess's mother opened her heart to her husband's children and they became a blended family despite distances.

Especially since her last parent's death, Bess continues to nurture her relationship with her stepsiblings, chatting regularly by phone. Bess is welcomed eagerly into their homes and tries to visit as often as possible even though she must travel halfway across the country to see them. Having these brothers and sisters in her life prevents her from experiencing the isolation that many only children have when their parents are gone. As Bess says, "If I didn't have them, I wouldn't have anybody."

Why We Discourage a Relationship

While Bess embraces her stepsiblings, there are midlife adults like Joan, who would rather not embrace or encourage a sibling relationship. There are endless reasons why we may shy away or reject a sibling after the last parent's death. One reason is that dependent siblings become even more dependent without parents to lean on. Joan feels quite strongly that she does not want to become a mother figure for her brother, who depended a great deal on their mother. Joan's brother was in the process of divorcing when their mother died and Joan acknowledges that he was in a great deal of pain. But Joan stresses that he had been floundering in his career and his personal life for a long time and she realized he would turn to her after their mother's death.

"I remember having that conscious awareness at some point

that things are going to shift. And sure enough, things have already shifted as Mike has tried to get in touch with more of the family. But I already have two children, I don't want to have another one," says Joan resolutely of her refusal to parent her brother.

Making a Sibling Relationship Work

In order for a fragile sibling relationship to survive, the siblings need to be willing to make changes. Perhaps in time, Joan will learn to set boundaries with her brother, as Ernie did with his brother who was dependent on their parents. While Ernie feels that his brother is now more self-sufficient than he was before their parents died, he still feels some responsibility for him. He is careful not to enable his brother's dependency. Their parents, loving and kind people, nonetheless were not able to put their foot down and continued to make loans to support their son's irresponsible lifestyle, denying his immaturity. The brothers now enjoy a healthier, more open and honest relationship—that is the reward for Ernie's firm hand and tacit way of encouraging his brother's independence.

Although Emma feels the need for stronger ties to her siblings, she is unwilling to compromise her emotional well-being to achieve that intimacy. Of her relationship with her six siblings, she remarks, "There are some that I don't think I'll ever have a relationship with. We're siblings but we don't particularly like each other."

After their father's death, several of the siblings decided to take an annual trip together. No spouses are invited; this holiday is just for the siblings. Having grown up with severely alcoholic parents, many of the sibs have been in recovery from alcoholism. They agreed that no drinking is permitted on these trips. Because of the ban on alcohol, some of the other brothers and sisters have refused to go along.

Of their decision, Emma says hopefully, "The trip gives us a sense of the family continuing. It's a very nice sense. Maybe as the others feel safer, they'll do it with us."

With this statement, Emma reminds us that relationships are not static. In her optimism is the acknowledgment that the changes brought by our shared loss of parents are ever evolving. Time, we remember, while moving faster now, is still the great healer.

The Spousal Relationship

As the loss of the last parent dredges up very deep-seated feelings and emotions, the relationship between spouses gets put to the test during this very trying bereavement period. According to Dr. Dana Cable, who has been counseling bereaved adults for more than twenty-five years, when a married adult loses the last parent, he or she often experiences some resentment of the spouse whose parents are still living.

Given the quirky and often irrational nature of emotions, this reaction isn't surprising. Hopefully, by the time we reach midlife, we are mature enough to refrain from acting on emotions but by no means are we necessarily in control of the way we feel. As baby boomers, we've digested psychology lingo that instructs us that "feelings are feelings, it's what you do with them that counts."

Cable cites an example of one of his cases in which the spouse whose last surviving parent died said, "I could never tell my husband this, but it's almost like I'm jealous. He still has his parents and I don't." This kind of resentment creates a strain on the marital relationship. When that happens, Cable explains that he has to get the other spouse in so both can talk about the feelings. He adds, "It's not like the wife wishes her in-laws were dead but it's still 'he has his parents and I don't have mine anymore.' "

What happens when our spouse disappoints us? For those who look for the comfort and support for which grieving begs, the spouse may come up short. Then we are left with anger or disillusionment. Jill confesses that when her last parent was dying, she found her spouse less supportive than she wished. With a demanding job that requires long hours, her husband wasn't able to be physically present much. As Jill says realistically, "There were a lot of ways I needed more support; maybe I needed so much, it wasn't possible."

But things have changed for the better. Jill and her husband were fortunate to have a pattern of good communication. She was able to express her disappointment and hurt to her husband in a way that he could hear. Since her mother's death, the couple has made adjustments that allow them to spend more time together. As Jill says, "Both of us are more aware of our own mortality now. It plays itself out in our relationship in some way." That "some way" is the determination to make their relationship better, now that there is a sense of the inevitability of the end of life. True, they probably have decades to go. But Jill and Carroll actively decided to give themselves the gift of more time together while they are still able to—a healthy response to Jill's loss.

Ronni also is making a healthy recovery from the loss of her parents, recognizing that their weaknesses do not have to be hers. For Ronni, the death of her last parent has brought dramatic changes in her relationship with her husband, a friend for nearly twenty years before they married. Lately, Ronni's focus has shifted from an emphasis on her career to an emphasis on creating a family with her spouse. She is now anxious to have children but she also feels the need to be more a part of her husband's family. Because of her history with her own severely dysfunctional and emotionally detached family, Ronni appreciates her husband's warm and loving, rather enmeshed family. Now, more than before her parents' deaths, she endeavors to sustain a close relationship to them. When she married, Ronni felt that her husband's family's unconditional love made him good "parenting" potential. As she approaches forty, Ronni wants very much to have children and to create with her spouse the loving family she did not have. With her increased awareness and appreciation of her husband's treasure of a family, Jill feels that her relationship with her husband has deepened since her last parent's death.

Much like Jill's gratitude for her in-laws, Sheila's husband came to her family with the adoration of a son-in-law whose own childhood was marred by the early divorce of his parents. Raised by a loving and caring mother at a time when there were few single mothers, Paul nonetheless grew up with a single parent who spent much of her time working to support her child. When Paul met Sheila, he embraced her large, extended family and was warmed by their immediate acceptance of him. According to Sheila, her husband adored her parents and was devastated by their deaths. "He can't, to this day, he cannot think about them, without crying." Sheila feels even closer to her husband since her father's death left her without parents. She worries about how he will feel when his own mother dies, and she fusses over him more than she did previously.

In fact, Sheila's reaction is one that I heard over and over again from spouses who had lost both parents. Seemingly gaining strength from their ordeal, these spouses shared a concern for the spouse whose parents were still living. Since his mother's death, Ross feels even closer to his wife, Catherine, who was his high school sweetheart. The relationship between mother-in-law and daughter-in-law had always been strained and was a source of discomfort for Ross. When his mother died, Ross saw that his wife was truly bereaved. He and Catherine began an honest dialogue and from that, Ross was able to see that his mother had created much of the friction. Despite the dissension, Catherine missed her mother-in-law, who had been so much a part of her life for so long. Ross recalls how supportive Catherine was when his father died nearly thirty years earlier. Her support after his mother's death was equally unwavering. Now he worries about how difficult it will be for Catherine when her own parents go. He shakes his head sadly and says, "My wife still has both parents and I think how much she'll have to go through. But everybody does, you can't beat this rap. We're all just passing through."

For Shelley, the death of her last parent came just as she and her husband, Morris, were beginning to empty the nest. With one child married and the other in college, the couple was spending more time with each other than they had in decades. Shortly after Shelley's mother died, Morris also lost his last parent. Not only did they have to restructure their relationship without children, this couple also had to redefine their relationship without parents to worry about. The transition has been relatively smooth for Shelley, who felt that her last parent's death was a transitional point for her. She decided to retire and redirect her professional life. She admits that the freedom from caring for a sick mother whose demands were draining has energized her. For now, she is pursuing her gardening and rowing, interests that she happily indulges. Shelley is also enjoying traveling internationally with Morris on his many business trips. Shelley and Morris realize that their own family unit and their children are their future. Life after parents is about looking forward.

Changes with Children

For many years, as I single-parented, my resentment at the lack of time I had to myself frequently spilled over to the kids. I'm not proud of that fact but it's true. There were no grandparents to pick up the slack or give me a break occasionally. Mom was too busy caring for my father. Occasionally, friends helped out. If I wanted to get out, I had to hire a babysitter, an expense I couldn't indulge in too frequently.

When my parents died, my resentment about my situation died with them. All that mattered was that time was slipping away. I wanted my children to experience the best of me so I worked to make our time together more positive. We took a vacation, the first in years. Not even a cold, constant downpour dampened our spirits as we trudged around historic Williamsburg in ponchos and wet socks. We saw every sight, shopped, ate out, ordered in, watched TV, swam in the hotel pool, and had a wonderful time with barely an argument in five days. It was a significant turning point.

Today, my relationship with my sons is better than ever. Andy and I argue over typical parent/teen issues—messy rooms, wet towels on the carpet, and lengthy showers—but basically, we co-exist in a loving, warm relationship. Now that Dan's away at college, our contact is limited to phone calls and e-mail. But when he's home, Dan sets aside time to spend with me. On my most recent campus visit, Dan arranged a dinner so I could meet his friends in his research group. The delight I experience from my children and the love and respect they return to me is an immeasurable reward for the altered perspective that came with the loss of my parents.

When Jean's last surviving parent finally died, Jean was jolted by the vulnerability she experienced, especially with regard to her children. But Jean wanted very much to keep her fears to herself and not to smother her children with her worries and concerns, as she felt her own mother often had done to her. Jean recognizes that many of the limits she places on herself, particularly around physical ability, are a direct result of her mother's worrying. Jean feels that it's important that she not inflict this same neurosis on her own children. She now encourages her children, to let them grow and have new experiences, often sublimating her own fears or concerns.

Brian is single and has no children. For many years, Brian was "afraid of kids," as he describes his feelings. That discomfort motivated him to become a Big Brother. Although his years of being a Big Brother were a confidence builder, it is largely because of his relationship with his girlfriend's son that Brian no longer feels uncomfortable or intimidated by being around kids. Since his father's death, Brian finds his dealings with Jimmy have changed for the better. Lately, Brian notices that he sounds more like his parents when he speaks to Jimmy. He also feels more nurturing.

Says Brian, "I heard myself telling him that education is important and explaining about the work ethic and how my parents instilled it in me. My mom went back and worked part-time in social work when I was in college but she never worked outside the home when I was growing up. She did volunteer work."

This parental aspect of himself that Brian is now experiencing comes somewhat as a surprise. Brian notes that his relationship with Jimmy's mother is the best relationship that he's ever had and he feels that it is moving forward and will probably become permanent, something that has eluded him until this point in his life. It is hard for Brian to pinpoint exactly what it is that made the difference but in his therapy since his last parent's death, Brian feels he has been able to confront disturbing demons from his past and to accept his parents' shortcomings. In doing so, Brian is moving on with his life, dumping childhood baggage that has inhibited his personal relationships. Clearly, for Brian, the death of his last parent was a significant turning point.

Cass feels the same way. Through most of her daughter's childhood, Cass wasn't able to show much physical affection, at least not the way she does now. While she considered her relationship with her own parents as "fairly easygoing," displays of affection from her parents were meager. Consequently, it's always been easier for Cass to be more affectionate with the students she taught than with her daughter. Soon after her daughter went off to college, Cass's last parent died. Suddenly Cass, who was divorced, was aware of the huge void that she faced. Depressed, she sought therapy. One of the things Cass learned during this time was that she "needed hugs." In fact, it was her daughter, whom Cass describes as "psychologically precocious," who confronted her about the lack of physical intimacy between them. Mother and daughter have worked to rectify the situation. "Now when I visit my daughter, I tell her what I need so that we make sure we get hugs," laughs Cass. Her daughter has enthusiastically responded. "I'm very blessed," declares Cass of this gratifying change in her life.

You recall that Jill and her husband made a conscious decision to spend more time together after Jill's last parent died. For Jill, this decision had implications reaching far beyond the immediate and obvious return. Jill and her husband used their time together to explore their longings and expectations regarding family life. One thing they realized was how much their son, Robby, had enjoyed the time alone with his dad while Jill was out of town caring for her dying mother. Jill was gratified that Carroll spent so much time with Robby even as she herself felt a lack of support from him. When Jill and Carroll reviewed that time in their lives, they realized that they were equally committed to giving their son the best of themselves. Out of those discussions emerged a decision to home school their eight-year-old son. The responsibility will fall largely on Jill but she is willing to take a hiatus from her accounting job, which she has found less satisfying in the past few years. The loss of income is worth the reward of spending more family time together. Jill and Carroll have reorganized their lives to create a child-centered home, quite different from the two-parent career family they were prior to the death of Jill's parents. They are looking forward to the challenges and changes.

Donna finds herself content and peaceful at midlife, although she is divorced and orphaned. With her son at the center of her life, Donna fills her days with activities and causes that reflect her parents' values. Since their deaths, she is even more content to keep her life simple and focused, much as they lived theirs. When Donna and her husband adopted their son as an infant, Donna didn't consider herself an "earth mother type." Yet, she remained a stay-at-home mom, indulging her love of people, cooking, and painting that have remained the mainstays of her life.

Donna comments, "People say to me, 'Now that you're divorced and your son is going off to college, you'll be free.' Everyone's reading into my life, but I'm already free. I've done everything I wanted. We used to say to my mother, 'Okay, all your chickens are home to roost now,' because that's what made her the happiest. And it's the same for me. I feel kind of sorry for my niece who has two kids and wants to stay home but she has to work full-time. Alberto knows that I'll be here for him. It's even more important because he was abandoned the first time. I think every kid needs to know someone is there for him all the time."

Jay always knew that someone was there for him. Growing up in a close-knit family, the emphasis was always on family and he and his sister were admonished to be loyal to each other. Jay has always encouraged a similar closeness in his own nuclear family. Yet, since the death of his last parent, Jay sensed a shift in the family base. Without visits to his parents to serve as the focal point for the family, it seemed that the family was growing apart. His kids were getting older and their interests were not organized around the family. But Jay wanted to maintain the family unit and felt emphatically that the family needed to pull together.

He explains, "About four or five years ago, I bought a ski chalet so that we could go skiing every weekend. We did that just to stay close as a family. It's very important to my daughter still. She's going to be nineteen. My son is not sure whether it's that important to him, but he's still kind of going his own way at sixteen. I think the four of us are stronger. I really do. We have to really, you know, go inward and do things together and be closer together. I think it makes us a stronger unit. We take a lot of vacations together."

As the death of the last parent makes its impact on us, it seems to affect our children also. Perhaps they sense our vulnerability. Perhaps they worry now that we are the oldest generation. Many children begin their own search to expand the family ties, as Mark's son has done.

Since his father died, Mark has noticed that his son, Todd, seems drawn to family in a way that he had not been previously. Just as Mark has sought out relatives since his parents' deaths, so is his grown son seeking to expand his family circle. This in turn forms an even stronger bond between father and son although they have always shared a warm relationship. Once a year, Todd now travels to Florida to visit his stepgrandparents. Now that his grandfather is dead, Todd has sought out his grandfather's brother, whom he never knew as a child. While in Florida, Todd also looked up his grandmother's brother. He picked him up and drove for two hours to take him to visit his sisters. Todd spent the day with his elderly relatives, chauffeuring them around, taking them out to eat, and enjoying their stories.

Mark says proudly of his son, "I think that he just likes the connection with family." Obviously, the acorn doesn't fall far from the tree in this family. Mark and his son share the desire for an extended family and they both are working at making that happen. The result is a deepening appreciation for each other's warmth and humanity.

Friends

"Make new friends but keep the old, one is silver and the other's gold." How many of us sang that round over and over in Scouts or at camp? Certainly, its meaning was different when we were ten and our friendships shifted weekly, depending upon who said what to whom. But by the time we reach midlife, although the song has been long forgotten, we have lived its words. Moving through life, we added to our collection of friends as though we were hoarding precious gemstones.

Friends are different from relatives. We choose our friends—we don't get them by default. True, we may keep in touch with childhood friends whom we've outgrown. Perhaps the friendship has been reduced to an annual exchange of holiday greetings but nevertheless it endures, driven by nostalgia. We have college friends we see once a decade and friends from our single days who know things about us we hope our children never discover. There are friends from the early days of our marriage, when we traded toilet-training tips and shared our dreams and plans. Some of us have predivorce friends and postdivorce friends, whose presence reminds us where we've been and where we're going. Some of our friends are former lovers. Some are sports buddies. We have friends from work, the people with whom we spend the majority of our days. Sometimes, it's not evident which friends are silver and which are gold.

But one thing is clear—at no time are friends more important than during a crisis. That's when we separate the blossoms from the weeds—the friends who rally around us, sharing our sorrow without really understanding it, plying us with food, and nurturing us through dark days. These are the friends who make time for us no matter what, who listen to us rant, rave and sputter, who wipe our tears and comfort us in their arms. Most importantly, these are the friends who don't forget us when the immediate crisis has passed—they are the ones we embrace forever after. They are the treasured friends of gold.

In the interviews I conducted, many midlife orphans addressed the issue of friendship. One of the outcomes of the death of the last parent is that we take stock of the quality of our friendships. As Brian explains, "I think it also has to do with what I want to do with the rest of my life, in the sense of what's important. The choice I'm making—which I probably wouldn't have made in the same way [prior to his last parent's death]—is to be with friends and family. I've got two old friends in Virginia—we were all resident advisors in a dorm. When I stopped going back home after my mother died, I started celebrating Christmas with the Wrights. I drove down to Virginia two weekends in a row, even though I hate to drive. I found the time to do it because it was something I wanted to do. And I saw my friend's father for the first time in thirty years."

Several of the adult orphans I interviewed spoke of new friendships with people they had met through their bereavement. One woman joined a bereavement group and discovered that another member of the group lived in a neighboring apartment. Through their intimate sharing, they have become good friends.

Ronni has reestablished a friendship with a woman she knew in graduate school. Both Ronni and her friend lost their fathers around the same time. Her friend's mother had died years before and, in the subsequent years, this woman also lost both of her siblings. Since Ronni's mother died, she has become closer to her friend, sharing some of the issues around the loss of parents. They are drawn together by their mutual loss but their friendship has grown beyond the loss to a mutually supportive and enjoyable relationship.

Miriam, on the other hand, is bothered by what seems like the insensitivity of her friends with regard to their own parents. "I think everybody has a different relationship with his or her parents. Mine wasn't so good because they made all the decisions for me, paid my bills, et cetera. I had to grow up when they got sick. I had to wake up fast. Maybe that's why I get freaked out when friends make negative comments about their parents. I used to do that but I know how much I miss mine. I really feel that I wish they would be easier on their parents."

For some of us, the workplace breeds friendships that offer support during a crisis. Midlife adults who spend most of their waking hours in an office frequently find that they bond with coworkers who are supportive during a crisis. For Ray, a forty-nine-year-old single man with no family in the vicinity, support from coworkers after his father's death has been very important.

Ray comments, "I think I have a group here that's been supersensitive, especially my secretary, who lost her husband and her father in six months' time. So she's had a sympathetic ear, and there's another woman whose mother had a problem similar to my mom's—she's been a source of comfort also. I think that there's a period of time when persons are incredibly giving to an individual and all of a sudden it just kind of wanes. But perhaps we need it more than when it first happened. Well, this group here has been really, really good to me. Our floor has had its share of tragedy here in the last few years. It seems like every one of the holidays brings some tragedy. Seems like we've all experienced these situations. I keep saying that these things can't continue. And I hope they don't. But since my dad died, I'm searching for answers and so it's always good to exchange opinions with another. It help clear up the maze—and I am in a maze. But my colleagues have been really wonderful."

The experience of becoming orphaned in midlife offers us the opportunity to be more compassionate toward our friends. Having gone through this wrenching experience, we are more empathetic when we see others walking the same path. As Portia remarks, "Now when a friend's parent dies, I feel so bad for them, knowing what a lonely feeling it is." Prior to her own parents' deaths, Portia couldn't understand the impact of the loss of the last parent.

But most importantly, we work harder at friendships now, making time for the friends we care so much about. Suddenly, we are no longer putting off that lunch date or the museum trip or even the quick cup of coffee. We begin to extend ourselves more to others. We divert the energy that we had placed on caretaking into our friends now. As the family unit shrinks, we expand our circle with friends. As Sarah explains, "Good friends are kind of replacing family."

Sometimes we are conflicted between spending holidays with friends or family. Often, after the death of the last parent, contact with family wanes. We find that friends reach out to include us for holiday meals. These are the people who become like family to us. We may no longer feel as close to relatives whose common thread was our parents. For instance, Sarah, who is divorced, still spends certain holidays with her aunt and uncle but she confesses that she doesn't particularly enjoy it anymore. Her own children, who do not live in the area, are usually not home for the holidays. Her cousins bring their spouses' siblings and their families and, for Sarah, the gathering no longer feels like "her family." Sarah celebrates other holidays with good friends—these are the times that she most enjoys.

"On the Jewish holidays and Thanksgiving, I'm still torn. This one friend, who's more like a sister, always comes to Rosh Hashanah here. At every family gathering I have, I include some friends. My daughter feels an obligation because she's not that far away but she's been in school and working and can't always come in. My son's too far away to come in very often. It would be so nice if I could have them here and re-create a family like my mother had."

With her children gone, Sarah has constructed holiday celebrations that revolve largely around her circle of close friends. Like many midlife adults who no longer have parents and who are not surrounded by a large extended family, Sarah focuses now on building relationships with the friends who have formed her family.

TAKING THE HELM

"She knew in her heart that nature has a preference for a particular order: parents die, then children die. But it was a harsh design, offering little relief from pain, for being in accord with it means that the fortunate find themselves orphaned."

—CHARLES FRAZIER, *Cold Mountain*

*O*ne of the first things I did after we closed up my parents' apartment was unearth the cardboard box of black-and-white photos that we'd found stowed away in their bedroom closet. From the hundred or so pictures, never before displayed, I chose about fifteen of my favorites. I selected some others from my own albums and bought frames for all of them. Today, this collection hangs in the long hallway off the foyer. Every time I go to and from the kitchen, I pass this gallery of memories.

As often as I've studied those pictures, I still find myself stopping to note some detail I've missed. For instance, there's the photo of my mother's parents standing proudly with their first grandson at his Bar Mitzvah. My grandmother is dressed in her finest hat and dress. It wasn't until someone asked about it, that I realized that she was wearing the black corrective oxfords that she always wore to alleviate her various foot ailments, the ones that my mother and I obviously inherited. Another photo, a sepia tone, shows my father and his siblings on the stoop outside their house, sporting identical Dutchboy haircuts, regardless of gender. There's the picture of my mother as a radiant young beauty. With her dark, full lips and a beret perched jauntily on her lustrous wavy pageboy, it's no wonder she was described as "the gorgeous Bert Ternoff" by the gossip columnist who noted my parents' engagement in the local paper. Still another shows Dad as a grad student, debonair in bow tie and spats, a devilish smile on his face as his arms encircle a nude sculpture in a Paris park.

But the photo that is dearest to me reveals a sweetly smiling toddler, hair parted in the center and pulled back in braids. This little girl was my parents' first daughter, who died before my sister Candy and I were born. I was ten years old before I learned of her existence. Mom and Dad, so private in their grief, refused to speak about Lynda Sue. When we were young, Candy and I waited for our parents to go out so we could run to the closet and sift through the forbidden and magical box of photos. We would study the pictures of Lynda Sue, so curious about this mystery child, yet always mindful of the tacit understanding that discouraged questions.

I used to spend a lot of time wondering about our relationship to the girl in the photos. Could we consider her our sister if we never knew her? If she hadn't died, would I have even been born? What would she be like had she lived? In my fantasies, of course, Lynda Sue was the perfect sister who would stick up for me and would never tease or poke fun at me. Because I couldn't ask about my deceased sister, I attributed great power to her. After all, in death she made quite an impact.

Decades later, Lynda Sue no longer remains an enigma. Her picture, hanging so publicly now, allows me to acknowledge and celebrate her brief life, something my parents were unable to do. Unveiling the ghost that affected us so subtly yet so powerfully all of those years mends the flaw in the documentation of our family's history. Giving Lynda Sue her rightful place in our family memoirs is what I like to think of as my first official act at the helm. It's up to us to pick and choose the memories to preserve and pass down. Having reached the helm, we become the bearers of our family history.

Preserving the Memories

When we are orphaned at midlife, we often find ourselves reaching out for something to connect us to what has been lost, because it's in these connections that we find peace and healing. Many of us begin to wonder a great deal about our family's past and it seems that no matter how many stories we have heard, they don't seem like nearly enough. Unless we have been conscientious observers and historians, once our parents are gone we regret how little we know about our history. Perhaps that's why my photo gallery means so much to me—it captures much of what I do remember. At the same time, the pictures prompt more questions than they answer. Did my father know his grandparents? How and why did his parents become so secularized? How long was my parents' courtship? I'm sorry that I don't have more details about the people and the stories that shaped my parents' lives.

How I envy Ernie, who had the foresight to audiotape his mother reminiscing about her life. Ernie created living history, just as my friend Ron did when he arranged for our friend Carol to videotape his mother in her final year, terminally ill with cancer. It's a wonderful documentary, one that could be dubbed "Chef Mimi: Cooking with Love." In it, Mimi describes how she prepares her family's most loved holiday foods—her fabulous chicken soup, her brisket smothered in rich gravy and onions, and their particular favorite, sweet and sour tongue. She recounts trivia (how her husband hated her cooking so, when they were newlyweds, she had to learn to cook like his mother) and the kind of details that you rarely find in cookbooks (you must use both kosher chicken and brisket for the soup and add parsnips to sweeten it). The video ensures that someday, Mimi's great-grandchildren (and perhaps their children, as well) will get to know this delightful woman in a way that they couldn't possibly from stories or photographs.

If you haven't recorded or documented much of your family's history, this is a good time to begin. You may want to start organizing archives, adding your personal papers, so that you can pass this information down to your own children one day. I've filed my parents' papers and whatever I found of my grandparents' in an accordion file—including birth certificates, war rationing cards, social security cards, *ketubahs* (Jewish marriage certificates), correspondence, and legal documents. I even found the menu and passenger list from the ship that carried my father to graduate school in England. Although my folks hardly seemed particularly sentimental about "things" (indeed, I was dismayed by the ease with which they disposed of so much when they sold our house thirty years ago), it was fascinating to discover that Dad had saved thirty-five years' worth of salary check stubs. My mother had kept decades' worth of letters. Every one of those corny little books I gave them was in a box. The flowery notes of love and gratitude I had inscribed are embarrassingly adolescent and excessive. But they serve to validate a relationship that was the way I like to remember it—basically loving and caring—although, God knows, we certainly had our trying times.

When my father died, someone suggested that we save the sympathy cards and letters that we received. I am eternally grateful for the suggestion. The notes are a window into how others perceived my parents—they reference my mother's warmth, compassion, and gracious hospitality and my father's sense of humor as well as his kind and generous nature. The cards and letters provide a treasure trove of others' memories and enable me to see my folks as unique individuals, not merely the mother and father I knew. I like to entertain the idea that someday my sons will read these and better understand who their grandparents were.

If you keep the sympathy notes and cards that you receive when your parents die, you will find it easier to know your parents not just as parents, but as individuals. For those adults who had troubled relationships with their parents, these notes help balance the perspective. Brian can't forget or discount his mother's alcoholism and emotional instability and his father's passiveness in dealing with his wife. But from the cards he received and the conversations he had with their friends and neighbors, Brian saw that there was another side to his parents. Other people's experience of his parents differed from his own; they spoke of qualities in them that Brian hadn't seen. Brian could have allowed his hurts and disappointment to color his memory of his parents. But by giving credence to what others had to say, he has been able to learn to accept his parents as the persons they were, flawed human beings who tried to love their only child in their own imperfect way.

Feeling the Changes

In the years since my parents have been gone, I've heard many midlife orphans remark that not a day goes by that they don't think of their parents. I can't say that is necessarily the case with me, but it's true that my folks are in my thoughts much of the time. I miss them and, even more, now that they are both deceased, I have begun to miss what our family was years ago, back before my father got sick. I miss his singing, his jokes, and his teasing. I miss schmoozing with my mom, one of us stretched out on the bed, the other showing off the haul from the latest Loehmann's spree. I miss family gatherings, back in the days when nobody worried about fat consumption and Mom's delicious rib roast with crispy browned potatoes was the standard fare, back before the tragedy, death, divorce, and schisms that diminished our clan.

I still hear my parents' voices, sometimes comforting me, other times admonishing and nagging, but now they don't resonate for long. Delia explains a similar phenomenon: "All my life when I was growing up, my mother was concerned that we associate with the right kind of people. I did whatever I wanted regardless; it's not that my mother ever stopped me from doing anything but now I'm a little more open. There's nobody saying anything in my ear, or at least I can ignore it now."

I agree. There's a certain heady freedom in being able to tune out those voices so easily now. Yet what I wouldn't give to pick up the phone and hear them once more, to listen to their reaction as I share the latest news about my kids. When my son Dan's college newspaper featured him in an article about undergraduates doing graduate research, how I longed to tell my parents, knowing how proud they would have been. Instead, I photocopied the article and distributed it to friends and family. And at this writing,

Andy's on a school exchange in Costa Rica, living with a non-English-speaking family. How thrilled (and worried—let's face it, my mother wasn't exactly adventurous) my parents would be at his moxie, especially my dad, who had once been fluent in Spanish and loved his own student travels abroad.

At times like these—when my children shine—I feel the loss of my parents acutely and it can still make me weepy. Gina, whose last parent died three years ago, shares this feeling. "It's hard to know that my parents won't be here when their grandchildren get married someday. And I wish they could see how well the kids are doing right now." And Jean, whose last parent died nearly seven years ago, wipes away tears as she speaks of watching her children grow up without her parents to witness their every achievement.

As midlife adults, we know the great pleasure our parents derived from their grandchildren and, indirectly, how that translated to validation for us. So when we remind our children how proud of them our parents would be, we continue to experience that praise, albeit indirectly. And even more, we nurture the connection to our parents just as they fostered in us the memories of our grandparents so that we had a sense of who our family was and where we had come from. It's also why I encourage my boys' relationship with their paternal grandparents, people to whom I was once very close. That family, too, has added texture to their lives, and as I see it, the more texture, the more interesting the quilt.

Knowing our roots gives shape and fullness to life. Once we're standing at the helm, with memories of our parents guiding us, we can prepare to fashion a course for the balance of our adulthood. In part, we are who we are because of who our parents were. But with the separateness that their deaths create, we are given an opportunity to redefine ourselves. Many of us turn inward at this time, with questions and doubts that belie our confidence and appearance of success. As our orphanhood becomes an accepted fact, it's time to integrate our legacy with the person we are going to be. In effect, we begin to tweak our self-image as we find ourselves in a new role at the helm of our family. Disagreeable traits from our parents that we see reflected in ourselves may now be cast aside once and for all. But even more, we can begin to clearly identify their virtues in ways that we could not previously. The measure of our parents' lives—their successes and failures—sets the standard for our own now.

That I can experience the essence of my parents so clearly at times, even after five years, continues to astonish me. I understand at last, at a gut level, that death is only the end of a physical life. We continue to think and talk about our parents for the rest of our lives, ensuring that their spirit lives on forever in our memories. Knowing how much my parents are still with me is of huge solace because I am certain now that I will be with my sons long after I'm physically gone. As we come face-to-face with our own mortality, this is the kind of knowledge that is quite comforting.

Taking Care of Ourselves

"I feel like I'm still young but every time I look in the mirror . . . well, that's not the young person I remember. You know how you try to tweak it. I'm still working on it, trying to get it to what I should look like."

George may be overreacting. At forty-five, he is fit and attractive. He confesses that he might be a bit "delusional" because he likes to think of himself as young. With no ailments to speak of, except for a few creaks here and there, George is in good health. Yet he can't forget his mother's warning: "Don't do what I did.

If you don't watch it, you'll gain five pounds every year and, before you know it, you'll be a blimp and you'll never know what happened to you. Don't let that happen to yourself."

George has always been fairly careful about his health but since his last parent's death he pays more attention to his exercising and diet regimen. George's father, a builder, was a strong man with well-developed muscles. But, according to George, he ate "the wrong stuff and drank too much beer," which resulted in a rather large belly. George feels that it's important to stay fit for his family and his future. His band now plays regularly for prominent charity balls, society weddings, and political functions. This demanding career and its success motivates George to work even harder at keeping himself fit and healthy, physically and emotionally.

Derek also finds that he is more into caring for himself now that he is at the helm. In some way, Derek feels that he's making up for lost time, that his own personal growth took off much later in life than for most adults. Overshadowed by his father when they worked together in the family business, Derek took a major step in establishing his own identity when he returned to school in his early fifties, after his father's death.

"I think I actually thrived after my parents died," Derek remarks candidly. "At first I struggled just to say, 'I've got to take care of myself now.' The grieving process is about getting rid of guilt and I'm doing that gradually. I'm growing up finally. I feel much more in touch with myself, more adult. Sometimes I feel like saying to my children, 'Stay in touch just because I love you, not because you owe it to me.' "

Derek adds that in the past few years since his last parent's death, he's become very aware of his own mortality. "Intellectually, I know there's no barrier now between me and death. I don't experience that emotionally. Instead, what I experience emotionally is the physical decline. I see a chiropractor for my back, my knees are bad, and I don't sleep well. I went to the hardware store the other day and I saw this guy with a big bald spot on the back of his head and said to myself, 'Do I look this way?' So I see all these aging processes and I'm very unhappy about it. People say I look great but I know I could die tomorrow. At sixty, I'm looking to make it to one hundred, although I know I'm really looking at probably fifteen real good active years ahead of me. So I'm going to put my sneakers on and get going, because after that, well. . . .''

The "well" that Derek concludes with is the same for each of us . . . it is the unknown. None of us can predict how or when our time will come. But once our last parent dies, there is no denying that, if nature takes its course, we're next. The previously unfathomable has become the inevitable. And so we begin to come to terms with our own mortality.

Dealing with Mortality

In an amusing tongue-in-cheek op ed piece that appeared in the *New York Times,* the author wrote of preparing for her and her husband's demise in order to mitigate the administrative burden of death for her children. Using her well-honed skills as a library director, she organized all of their personal information on computer to help their kids sort out everything—a listing of assets, complete with account numbers; deed to the house; insurance records; medical proxies; even suggestions for memorial services. With little difficulty, she produced a complete database, but found that she was stumped when she tried to give the file a name: "Dead Parents File" seemed too direct and "346.052," the Dewey Decimal System number for books dealing with death, wouldn't mean much to her offspring. After much deliberation, she finally settled on calling her file "Good Grief!"[39]

I chuckled as I read this article—it helps to have a sense of humor once you start thinking about your own mortality. And as we age, it's only natural to begin to think about death. While it may be possible to stave off serious thoughts of mortality for a fairly long time, once we take the helm from our parents, there's no way to avoid it. Coping with the loss of our parents forces us to confront concrete issues about the end of life. Adult children now feel compelled to put our own financial and business matters in order. The burden of handling matters—medical directives, burial site, funeral details, estate and financial matters—under the pressure of grief and time constraints make it clear that one of the kindest things you can do for your family is to take care of these things before you die.

After watching my parents experience terrible suffering, I saw that the need for a living will was obvious but I kept procrastinating. I'd had a will since my first son was born, and had updated it several times through the years, but I had yet to sign a living will, the simple document that directs end-of-life choices. Unfortunately, my father had no living will and, as a result, was resuscitated when he aspirated. This emergency move prolonged his near-vegetative state for several more agonizing weeks. My mother wanted to be sure nothing like that happened to her. She signed a living will in the hospital, right before she underwent her brain biopsy. We recruited a man who was visiting a relative in the next room to stand in as a witness.

It wasn't until two years after my mother's death that I was finally able to sign my living will. For me, taking such a step felt like an admission of my vulnerability. It made my own mortality a reality. I had struggled, telling myself I was being silly, yet for two years I ignored the document that sat in a file on my desk.

What made me finally do it? I'm not sure, but it could have been the obituary I saw about a divorced woman, about my age, who left behind three adolescent children. I thought, "Oh, those poor kids, so young to have to make all those decisions." When I finally signed, it was an enormous relief to know that my living will would alleviate the burden of my children having to make heart-wrenching decisions without my input. Signing my living will let me feel more adult, more in control of my life, knowing that I had some say in how it should end.

Our rise to the helm prompts us to deal with end-of-life matters. It's time to think about the kind of burial we want, draw up a will and a living will, purchase a cemetery plot, and put our finances in order. If our children are old enough, we must talk to them about our end-of-life wishes. It's not morbid, it's smart. In a society that pours out the most personal problems on national television talk shows, it's interesting that we find it as uncomfortable to speak with our children about our finances as it is to discuss our fears.

Honoring Our Parents

As we have seen, the period after our last parent dies is frequently a time of intense self-examination as we review who our parents were and how that has affected us. But there is a larger purpose to this introspection. In her book *Death: The Final Stage of Growth,* Elisabeth Kübler-Ross reminds us that the search for self is the ultimate goal of growth. She writes that by reaching out and committing ourselves to others, we can begin to transcend our individual existence. "And through a lifetime of such commitment, you can face your final end with peace and joy, knowing that you have lived your life well."[37]

We need to know who we are so we can assess where we want to go. As adults, few of us have lived for ourselves alone. In some way, we have shared ourselves with others, through our work and through our relationships with family and friends. However, as we recover from the death of our last parent and it is now perfectly clear that our lives have a finite season, we may experience an urgency to commit ourselves to something larger. This is the time when midlife adults begin to reshape our lives to fit new circumstances. Some of us redirect our careers. Some find new relationships. Some find a resurgence of creative energy and discover new passions or hobbies.

One of the ways in which many of us honor our parents' memory is through charity work and volunteerism. The year after my father died, I participated in my first Alzheimer's Walk with the Southeastern Pennsylvania chapter of the Alzheimer's Association. For the next couple of years, my sons and I joined thousands for this wonderful annual event that raises money for research on this disease. We solicited friends for contributions. When Dan went off to college, a group of friends joined me and we walked the length of Kelly Drive together, enjoying the beautiful Sunday morning. Each year since my mother's death, I have been a block leader for the American Cancer Society. It takes only a few hours of my time but by participating in this way, I honor my parents in ways that would make them proud, in ways that are productive and helpful to a world sorely in need.

The midlife orphans I interviewed found creative ways to honor their parents. For example, Olga, a fundraiser, organized a dance scholarship for college students because it reflected a particular interest of hers. Gina and her siblings also set up a scholarship for Catholic high school students in her parents' memory, knowing that her parents, who were very religious, would be pleased. Some adults planted memorial gardens. Others began doing volunteer work with organizations similar to ones with which their parents had also volunteered.

Changing Rituals and Traditions

One aspect of taking the helm is in establishing new traditions and rituals to reflect our altered relationships and circumstances. As sad as the first holidays are without our parents, the traditions we create now may, in the long run, turn out to be more satisfying because we are no longer bound to rigid family customs. Sarah illustrated this recently when she related a personal story to me.

Several years ago, at the approach of the first Jewish New Year since both of her children had left home, Sarah found herself growing increasingly depressed. Orphaned for several years at that point, she was missing her parents terribly and fretting over the notion that she and her husband would be spending the holiday alone. Sarah had little energy to cook but she wanted desperately to celebrate the holiday with a circle of loved ones, so she decided to invite friends for a potluck dinner. Initially, she felt uncomfortable about asking people to bring food for a holiday dinner— this wasn't how her mother had done it. But the gathering was a huge success and has become an annual event. And each year the guest list expands. The menu is largely vegetarian, a far cry from the brisket, potatoes, and starchy dishes that dominated her parents' traditional holiday table. Sarah and her husband celebrate the holiday with a menu that reflects their own lifestyle and that of their friends. Sarah has integrated her parents' observation of the religious holiday with her own values. She has taken the helm with aplomb.

Prescription for Growth

Throughout this book, we have walked through the steps that we must complete if we are to move on after our parents die. We have seen how midlife orphans examine the past, recalling both meaningful and unpleasant memories. We have met adults who had to learn to acknowledge feelings about their parents and internalize them. Finally, we have seen how we must make conscious decisions to move on, if only with tiny, tentative steps until we find comfort in our own shoes, shoes that fit us better than those of our parents. As Margot says, "With Mom gone, it's like all at once I was forced to grow up a second time. One is kind of a command performance and one is a privilege. I regret that it took Mom dying to bring that about. So, there's good stuff about her I miss and there's a lot of stuff I don't miss. It's a real dilemma."

The dilemma is one that Margot is solving by solidifying her relationship with her husband and stepchildren. She is making career decisions based on what is good for her and her family. She has rejected her mother's conventional social concerns but, at the same time, she is learning to integrate her parents' values with her own. In making these changes in her life, Margot is gaining a deepening appreciation for her parents.

What is happening to Margot is what happens to all of us as we make the transition from adult child to truly adult at last. Two years after her last parent's death, Allie eloquently reflects, "My parents gave me innumerable material gifts but, more importantly, they gave me inner gifts, a certain kind of tradition, a value system, and an ethical system. They were examples to me. I've been able to take the best of them over many, many years. I've had to sift and sort and set boundaries and decide what to keep and what to let go of. I've had to find a way to weave a web that feels like nothing but gratitude."

Like Allie, midlife orphans will navigate through uncharted rivers of change until we find peace with our parents and with ourselves. As we step to the helm, this becomes our course.

BIBLIOGRAPHY

Akner, Lois. F., C.S.W., with Catherine Whitney. *How to Survive the Loss of a Parent: A Guide for Adults*. New York: William Morrow, 1993.

Anderson, Patricia. *Affairs in Order: A Complete Resource Guide to Death and Dying*. New York: Macmillan, 1991.

Angel, Marc. *The Orphaned Adult: Confronting the Death of a Parent*. New York: Insight Books, 1987.

Beisser, Arnold R. *A Graceful Passage*. New York: Doubleday, 1990.

Bond, Alma H. *On Becoming a Grandparent: A Diary of Family Discovery*. Bridgehampton, NY: Bridge Works Publishing, 1994.

Bradshaw, John. *Homecoming: Reclaiming and Championing Your Inner Child*. New York: Bantam Books, 1990.

Brener, Anne. *Mourning and Mitzvah: A Guided Journal for Walking the Mourner's Path through Grief to Healing*. Woodstock: Jewish Lights Publishing, 1993.

Bricklin, Barry Ph.D., and Patricia Bricklin. *Strong Family, Strong Child: The Art of Working Together to Develop a Healthy Child*. New York: Delacorte Press, 1970.

Brody, Elaine M. "Parent Care As a Normative Family Stress." *Gerontologist*, vol. 25, 1985.

Brody, Jane. "Personal Health." *New York Times* (September 23, 1987).

Cooney, Teresa M. and Peter Uhlenberg. "Support from Parents over the Life Course: The Adult Child's Perspective." *Social Forces,* vol. 71: 1, September 1992: 63–84.

Dane, Barbara Oberhofer. "Middle-aged Adults Mourning the Death of a Parent." *Journal of Gerontological Social Work*, vol. 14 (3/4) 1989: 75–89.

Datan, N., and N. Lohmann, eds. *Transitions of Aging*. New York: Academic Press, 1980.

Doehlemann, Martin. "The Death of the Last Parent As the Developmental Turning Point in the Lifetime of an Adult." *Zeitschrift fur Sozialisationsforschung und Erziehungssoziologie*. 7,3 (1987): 178–96.

Donnelly, Katherine Fair. *Recovering from the Loss of a Parent*. New York: Berkley Books, 1993.

Douglas, Joan Delahanty. "Patterns of Change Following Parent Death in Midlife Adults." *OMEGA*, vol. 22 (2, 1990–91): 123–137.

Edelman, Hope. *Motherless Daughters*. New York: Dell Publishing, 1994.

Edmonson, Brad. "The Future of Spending." *American Demographics* (January 1995):12–19.

Elias, M. "The New Midlife Crisis." *Longevity* 4(9) (August 1992): 72–74, 90.

Fitzgerald, Helen. *The Mourning Handbook*. New York: Simon & Schuster, 1994.

Fosler, R. Scott. "Demographics of the 90s: The Issues and Implications for Public Policy." *Vital Speeches of the Day,* vol. 55, #18 (July 1, 1989): 572–76.

Frazier, Charles. *Cold Mountain.* New York: Atlantic Monthly Press, 1997.

Friday, Nancy. *My Mother/My Self.* New York: Dell, 1987.

Ginott, Haim G. *Between Parent and Child: New Solutions to Old Problems.* New York: Macmillan, 1965.

Golden, Thomas R. *Swallowed by a Snake: The Gift of the Masculine Side of Healing.* Kensington: Golden Healing Publishing, 1996.

Grollman, Earl A. *Explaining Death to Children.* Boston: Beacon Press, 1967.

Grollman, Earl A., ed. *Time Remembered: A Journal for Survivors.* Boston: Beacon Press, 1987.

Grollman, Earl A., ed. *What Helped Me When My Loved One Died.* Boston: Beacon Press, 1982.

Gross, A. "A Matter of Wills." *Ladies' Home Journal.* (February 1995): 92–95.

Hall, Calvin S., and Vernon J. Nordby. *A Primer of Jungian Psychology.* New York: Taplinger, 1973.

Hawkins, Anne Hunsaker. "Constructing Death: Three Pathographies about Dying," *OMEGA,* vol. 22(4) (1990–91): 301–317.

Hillman, James. *The Soul's Code: In Search of Character and Calling.* New York: Random House, 1996.

James, John W., and Frank Cherry. *The Grief Recovery Handbook.* New York: Harper & Row, 1988.

Kalish, Richard A., ed. *Midlife Loss: Coping Strategies.* Newbury Park: SAGE Publications, 1989.

Kaltreider, Nancy B. M.D., Terry Becker, M.D. and Mardi J. Horowitz, M.D. "Relationship Testing after the Loss of a Parent." *American Journal of Psychiatry,* 141:2 (February 1984): 243–46.

Kennedy, Alexandra. *Losing a Parent.* New York: HarperCollins, 1991.

Kreisman, Jerold J., M.D. and Hal Straus. *I Hate You—Don't Leave Me: Understanding the Borderline Personality.* New York: Avon Books, 1989.

Kübler-Ross, Elisabeth. *Death: The Final Stage of Growth.* Englewood Cliffs, NJ: Prentice Hall, 1975.

Kübler-Ross, Elisabeth. *Living with Death and Dying.* New York: Macmillan, 1981.

Kübler-Ross, Elisabeth, M.D. *On Death and Dying.* New York, Macmillan, 1969.

Kushner, Harold S. *How Good Do We Have to Be? A New Understanding of Guilt and Forgiveness.* Boston: Little, Brown, 1996.

Kutner, Lawrence. "Parent and Child." *New York Times* (April 1, 1993).

Levine, Stephen. *Healing into Life and Death.* Berkeley, CA: Celestial Arts, 1991.

Marshall, Fiona. *Losing a Parent.* Tucson, AZ: Fisher Books, 1993.

McCulloch, Meredith. "One Mother's Farewell File," *New York Times* (April 15, 1998).

Moss, Miriam S., Sidney Z. Moss, Robert Rubinstein, and Nancy Resch. "Impact of Elderly Mother's Death on Middle-age Daughters." *International Journal of Aging and Human Development,* vol. 37(1) (1993): 1–22.

Moss, Miriam S. and Sidney Z. Moss. "The Impact of Parental Death on Middle-aged Children," *OMEGA,* vol. 14 (1) (1983–84): 65–75.

Myers, Edward. *When Parents Die: A Guide for Adults.* New York: Viking, 1986.

Nuland, Sherwin B. *How We Die: Reflections on Life's Final Chapter.* New York: Alfred A. Knopf, 1994.

O'Connor, Nancy. *Letting Go with Love: The Grieving Process.* Tucson, AZ: La Mariposa Press, 1986.

Peck, M. Scott, M.D. *Denial of the Soul: Spiritual and Medical Perspectives on Euthanasia and Mortality.* New York: Harmony Books, 1997.

Rando, Therese A. *Treatment of Complicated Mourning.* Champaign, IL: Research Press, 1993.

Rapoport, Nessa. *A Woman's Book of Grieving.* New York: William Morrow, 1994.

Rosenblatt, Paul, and Carol Elde. "Shared Reminiscence about a Deceased Parent: Implications for Grief Education and Grief Counseling." *Family Relations,* vol. 39, #2 (April 1990): 206–10.

Rosenfeld, Jeffrey P. "Old Age, New Heirs." *American Demographics,* vol. 14 (May 1992): 46–49.

Rubin, Bonnie Miller, and Terry Wilson. "Baby Boomers Are Looking at Heirlooms and Seeing Dollar Signs." *Philadelphia Inquirer* (October 24, 1997).

Sandmaier, Marian. *Original Kin: The Search for Connection among Adult Sisters and Brothers.* New York: Dutton, 1994.

Saunders, Laura, ed. "Gravy Boat Diplomacy," *Forbes,* (October 20, 1997) 306–308.

Schiff, Harriet S. *Living through Mourning: Finding Comfort and Hope When a Loved One Has Died.* New York: Viking Penguin, 1986.

Schoenberg, B., ed. *Anticipatory Grief.* New York: Columbia University Press, 1974.

Scileppi, Kenneth P. *Caring for the Parents Who Cared for You: What to Do When an Aging Parent Needs You.* Secaucus, NJ: Carol Publishing Group, 1996.

Shaie, K. Warner, and Sherry L. Willis. *Adult Development and Aging (Fourth Edition).* New York: HarperCollins College Publishers, 1996.

Sheehy, Gail. *New Passages, Mapping Your Life across Time*. New York: Random House, 1995.

Sheehy, Gail. *Passages*. New York: Bantam, 1977.

Silverstein, Olga, and Beth Rashbaum. *The Courage to Raise Good Men*. New York: Viking, 1994.

Staudacher, Carol. *Men and Grief*. Oakland, CA: New Harbinger Publications, 1991.

Stearns, Ann Kaiser. *Coming Back: Rebuilding Lives after Crises and Loss*. New York: Random House, 1988.

Swigert, Jane. *The Myth of the Bad Mother: The Emotional Realities of Mothering*. New York: Doubleday, 1991.

Troll, Lillian E., and Sheila J. Miller. *Families in Later Life*. Belmont, CA: Wadsworth: 1979.

Umberson, Debra, and Meichu D. Chen. "Effects of a Parent's Death on Adult Children: Relationship Salience and Reaction to Loss," *American Sociological Review*. vol. 59, 1994 (February) 152–168.

Veninga, Robert. *A Gift of Hope: How We Survive Our Tragedies*. New York: Ballantine, 1986.

Viorst, Judith. *Necessary Losses*. New York: Fawcett Gold Medal, 1987.

Viorst, Judith. "No One Loved You More." *Redbook*. (November 1993): 68.

Volkan, Vamik D., M.D., and Elizabeth Zintl. *Life after Loss: the Lessons of Grief*. New York: Charles Scribner's Sons, 1993.

Walsh, Froma, and Monica McGoldrick, eds. *Living beyond Loss*. New York: Norton, 1991.

Weenolsen, Patricia. *The Art of Dying: How to Leave This World with Dignity and Grace, at Peace with Yourself and Your Loved Ones.* New York: St. Martin's Press, 1996.

Wolfelt, Alan D. *Understanding Grief: Helping Yourself Heal.* Bristol, Penna: Accelerated Development, 1992.

Zal, H. Michael. *The Sandwich Generation: Caught between Growing Children and Aging Parents.* New York: Insight Books, 1992.

ENDNOTES

[1]Myers, Edward. *When Parents Die: A Guide for Adults*. New York: Viking, 1986, p. 5.

[2]Moss, Miriam S., and Sidney Z. Moss. "The Impact of Parental Death on Middle Aged Children," *OMEGA*, vol. 14(1), 1983–84, p. 66.

[3]op. cit., Moss, Miriam S., and Sidney Z. Moss, p. 66.

[4]A.D. Weisman, "Is Mourning Necessary?" in *Anticipatory Grief*, B. Schoenberg (ed.), New York: Columbia University Press, NY, 1974, p. 15.

[5]Ginott, Dr. Haim G. *Between Parent and Child: New Solutions to Old Problems*. New York: The Macmillan Company, NY, 1965. p. 144

[6]op. cit. Moss, Miriam S. and Sidney Z. Moss, "The Impact of Parental Death on Middle Aged Children," *OMEGA*, Vol. 14(1), 1983–84, p.70

[7]Angel, Rabbi Marc D., *The Orphaned Adult: Confronting the Death of a Parent*. New York: Human Sciences Press Inc., 1987, p.44.

[8]Dane, Barbara Oberhofer. Middle-Aged Parents Mourning the Death of a Parent, *Journal of Gerontological Social Work*, Vol. 4 (3/4) 1989, p.78

[9]Hall, Calvin S. and Vernon J. Nordby, *A Primer of Jungian Psychology*, New York: Taplinger Publishing Co., 1973, p. 92.

[10]Hawkins, Anne Hunsaker. "Constructing Death: Three Pathographies About Dying," *OMEGA*, Vol. 22 (4) 1990–91, p. 301.

[11]Wolfelt, Alan D. *Understanding Grief: Helping Yourself Heal*. Bristol, Penna: Accelerated Developed, 1992.

[12]Doehlemann, Martin. "The Death of the Last Parent as the Developmental Turning Point in the Lifetime of an Adult," (trans). *Zeitschrift fur Sozialisationsforschung und Erziehungssoziologie* 7,3 (1987): 178–96.

[13]Horowitz, M. J., Krupnick, J., Kaltrieder N., Wilner, N., Leong, A., & Marmar, R.C. "Initial Psychological Response to Parental Death," *Archives of General Psychiatry*, 38, pp.316–323.

[14]Rosenblatt, Paul and Carol Elde, p. 208.

[15]Saunders, Laura, ed. "Gravy Boat Diplomacy," *Forbes Magazine*, October 20, 1997, pp. 306–8.

[16]Sandmaier, Marian. *Original Kin: The Search for Connection Among Adult Sisters and Brothers.* New York: Dutton, 1994. p. 197.

[17]Rubin,Bonnie Miller and Terry Wilson. *The Philadelphia Inquirer,* October 24, 1997. (Reprinted from *Chicago Tribune*)

[18]Bell, Bryan. *Lessons in Lifemanship,* Chapter 12: The Family Inheritance, p. 3. Retrieved November 13, 1997 from the World Wide Web: http://bbll.com/ch12.html

[19]Rosenfeld, Jeffrey P. "Old Age, New Heirs," *American Demographics,* vol. 14, no. 5 (May 1992) p.46.

[20]op. cit. Dane, Barbara Oberhofer, *"Middle-Aged Adults Mourning the Death of a Parent,"* p.77.

[21]Kreisman, Jerold J., M.D., & Hal Straus, *I Hate You—Don't Leave Me: Understanding the Borderline Personality,* New York: Avon Books, 1989, p. 49.

[22]Viorst, Judith. *Necessary Losses.* New York: A Fawcett Gold Medal Book, Ballantine Books, 1986, p.35.

[23]Hillman, James. *The Soul's Code: In Search of Character and Calling.* New York: Random House, 1996, p. 165.

[24]Umberson, Debra and Meichu D. Chen. "Effects of a Parent's Death on Adult Children: Relationship Salience and Reaction to Loss," *American Sociological Review,* 1994, Vol. 59, February, pp. 152–169. p. 153

[25]Troll, Lillian E. "Intergenerational Relations in Later Life: A Family System Approach." In N. Datan & N. Lohmann, (eds), *Transitions in Aging.* New York: Academic Press, 1980, p. 84.

[26]Cooney, Teresa .M., and Peter Uhlenberg. "Support from Parents over the Life Course: The Adult Child's Perspective," *Social Forces,* 7 (1), pp.63–84.

[27]op. cit., Cooney, Teresa .M., and Peter Uhlenberg.

[28]Brody, E.M., "Parent Care as a Normative Family Stress," *Gerontologist,* vol. 25, 1985, pp.19–29.

[29]Shaie, K. Warner and Sherry L. Willis. *Adult Development and Aging, Fourth edition.* New York: Harper Collins College Publishers, 1996, p. 162.

[30]Op. cit, Shaie, K. Warner and Sherry L. Willis. p.85

[31]Brody, Elaine M. "Parent Care as a Normative Family Stress," *Gerontologist,* (vol. 25 #1) 1985, pp. 19–29.

[32]Rosenblatt, Paul and Carol Elde, "Shared Reminiscence about a Deceased Parent: Implications for Grief Education and Grief Counseling," *Family Relations,* 39, April 1990, p. 208.

[33]Bradshaw, John. *Homecoming: Reclaiming and Championing Your Inner Child.* New York: Bantam Books, 1990, p. 65.

[34]Silverstein, Olga and Beth Rashbaum. *The Courage to Raise Good Men.* New York: Viking, 1994, p.216.

[35]Viorst, Judith. *Necessary Losses.* A Fawcett Gold Medal Book, New York: Ballantine Books, 1996, p.73.

[36]Edelman, Hope. *Motherless Daughters,* New York: Dell, p. xxxiii.

[37]Bricklin, Barry, Ph.D. and Patricia Bricklin. *Strong Family, Strong Child: The Art of Working Together to Develop a Healthy Child.* New York: Delacorte Press, 1970, p. 3.

[38]Edelman, Hope. *Motherless Daughters,* p. 201

[39]McCullough, Meredith. "One Mother's Farewell File," *New York Times,* p.A25, April 15, 1998.

[40]Kübler-Ross, Elisabeth. *Death: The Final Stage of Growth.* Englewood Cliffs, Prentice-Hall, 1975, p. 145.

INDEX